104742

MW01104226

Footprints & Fragrance in the
Outback

DATE DUE

12/Feb 19+hy

July 22 /.2

ALLIANCE CHURCH
LIBRARY

Footprints & Fragrance In the Outback

Aborigines?

Australia?

They'd never heard of either.

They were an ordinary couple living the "American Dream" of a house, kids, pets and work.

Bob and Ethel Stewart never dreamt how drastically their lives would change, nor would they live to know the full impact they would have on so many lives.

A stunned Aboriginal Affairs government official, while touring the vast inland area, learned a secret. Bob and Ethel are not only remembered, half a century after leaving, but are still highly revered by aborigines in the outback of Western Australia.

Because of their obedience in following God's leading and their love for the aboriginal people, in many inland areas where Bob and Ethel never made a single footprint, the fragrance of a loving God has flown.

The following story contains glimpses, both exciting and otherwise; of real life events that took place during the eighteen years the Stewarts lived and worked in the outback/inland area of Western Australia with stone-age Spinifex tribes.

We hope these stories will enrich your life as you witness God's faithfulness to a couple of His servants.

Marilyn Stewart
Email: childoftheoutback@juno.com

ISBN 0-7414-1922-X

Cover art by Cathi A. Wong
E-mail: caw004@aol.com

Published by:

PUBLISHING.COM

519 West Lancaster Avenue
Haverford, PA 19041-1413
Info@buybooksontheweb.com
www.buybooksontheweb.com
Toll-free (877) BUY BOOK
Local Phone (610) 520-2500
Fax (610) 519-0261

Printed in the United States of America

Printed on Recycled Paper

Published February 2004

Other titles by this author:

Child of the Outback

Acknowledgements

Thanks to the readers of my first book - you encouraged me to try writing yet another.

Bob and Kat Emmelkamp I am grateful for your repeated assistance regarding my various computer problems.

Linda Edstrom, Carolyn Galarza, and Ted Taft, thank you for your valuable assistance, input, reading and rereading.

Roger Green, Brian & Dawn Hadfield your inputs were so very helpful as well as timely.

Darlene Kingi, the dearest of sisters. Generous with pertinent information, help in tightening up my sentences, suggestions, editing with care, and so very supportive. You are a jewel.

Kathy Peterson – I so appreciate your help, knowledge, and editing skills. Thanks for that timely note of encouragement, which returned my audacity to finish writing this book.

Cathi Wong, the cover artist of this book – as well as on *"Child of the Outback"* – GREAT JOB!

Without the numerous loyal prayer supporters there is no way humanly possible that our family would have endured if it had not been for your faithfulness.

My deepest appreciation and thanks to my longsuffering husband John. He not only encouraged me to write, but also worked on the photos so I could just drop them in place.

Last but certainly not least our Pomeranians, Cinco and Seis for their insistence that I take play breaks – with them!

Dedication

In memory of Bob and Ethel Stewart and traditional aborigines of the Western Australian outback, with whom they lived, loved and labored.

Special thanks to the following individuals and/or relatives who allowed me to share events from their lives.

Wilbur Brooks
Jerry Jamieson
Jimmy Mardi
Don Sinclair
Willy Stewart
Carlene Anderson West

I am so thankful to have known each of you and am forever richer in spirit due to the impact you and your kin have had on my life.

This book could not have been written without the generous assistance given to me by my sister Darlene Kingi, and brothers, Dale and Stephen Stewart.

The Stewart family hopes you will be encouraged and strengthened by these stories, to live your own life and dreams.

The cover photo is the actual road made by Bob's tire tracks on an inland trip. The man in the cameo is Jerry whose story is told in chapter twelve - Jerry & Journey.

Western Australia

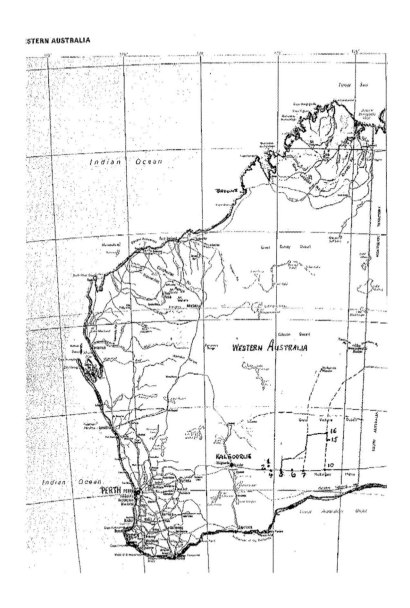

1. Cundeelee 2. Coonana 4. Zanthus 6. Naretha
7. Rawlina 10. Loongana 16. Tjuntjuntjara

Table of Contents

Background & Book

Two Thousand and One arrived marking eight years since I had been "home" and a year since my book *Child of the Outback* had rolled off the presses. In that book I mentioned my sister was writing a book of stories about our folks and the Spinifex aborigines which had taken place during this same time period and at the same location, but that she just hadn't finished it yet.

I had recently begun to feel strongly that it was time to return yet again to my roots in the outback of Western Australia. Home is in the real outback where aborigines, red dirt, long distances, short-wave radios, flying doctors, no shops, the scarcity of water, and only an occasional visitor, are still the common denominators.

My earliest memories are of interacting with aborigines. As a six year old, I had quickly absorbed their culture and ways. Since I had grown up in their society, I had lived under the influence of their laws, and identified myself as one of them.

The eagles are strong and swift with wingspans of five to eight feet. Red and gray kangaroo number in the high millions. Emu and wild camels like traveling and sleeping on the graded fire break rather than on dry vegetation or amongst the needle-like spinifex and dingoes prowl lurking not far behind them.

The only road available to get back into the area where I would need to go was via a once graded (in 1993) firebreak, which at times runs next to the dingo fence.

I had many reasons for going "down under" once again, with the main thought that of renewing family ties. My younger brother had recently remarried and I was looking forward to meeting this "treasure" in his life.

Another very strong longing, almost to the point of a compulsion, was to return and reconnect with "my people," and revisit Coonana and Cundeelee. I desired to see the Aboriginal Community at Tjuntjuntjara, where my brother was currently working.

I figured since I would already be down under and relatively close to New Zealand, I would stop over for a few days. I could not only see my Mum, who is in a nursing home there, but also while visiting my sister and her children, prod her a bit regarding her unfinished book.

My journey began March 2002 with a drive to the airport in Phoenix, continued via airplanes to Los Angeles, Sydney, across to Perth in Western Australia, and finally ended nearly 500 hundred miles inland at Kalgoorlie.

After all of that flying it was good to be back on firm ground - even when it meant bouncing along a dirt track for a further 425 miles. Due to my lost luggage, and a heavy rainfall an hour after my arrival, we stayed two nights in Kalgoorlie instead of just a couple of hours. We hoped the track would dry so that we wouldn't get stuck in the mud.

Finally, we were headed inland into the true outback. Sitting up so high in the cab of the Aboriginal Community's diesel powered truck, we had a great view, bounced continually, and could hardly hear what the other was shouting. With my brother, Stephen, at the wheel of the Tjuntjuntjara Community 4x4, the drive took us a mere ten hours, in which we were given only two quick (bush) bathroom breaks. He told me early on that this was a supply run and not a photo shoot – no stopping for pictures – period.

Stephen took charge of my re-introduction to the aboriginal community. Upon arrival, he took me to where I was going to stay, and left after saying, "get unpacked and have a cuppa while I go and unload the supply truck." I dearly wanted to go watch/help – just be there during the unpacking to see what all we had brought in, but knew I was in another world. According to protocol and in order to not offend anyone, for now, I would have to stay inside.

Later that evening, after Stephen had come back and had his "cuppa" we heard a slight noise outside at which Stephen hollered out a welcome. In walked six older men and one by one as Stephen spoke their name they hesitantly walked over to me and very gently clasped my hand between the two of theirs and looked deep into my eyes.

As my smile widened in delight over their welcome, the atmosphere lightened. Glancing at Stephen and checking to see if we had enough mugs, I asked if they would like a cuppa. A sigh of relief went up as they relaxed knowing I had not changed, was happy to be home, and willing to eat/share with them. In the following days, I was invited by the people to sit on the ground next to them and chat.

I had a fabulous time sitting on the red dirt under various shade trees, renewing old ties and making new friends among the Spinifex aborigines.

All too soon, it was time to leave and visit family in New Zealand. It was only towards the end of my delightful stay with Darlene that an added reason for this trip became apparent. After much talking and sharing together, we realized she was struggling with much more than simply sitting down and typing out events and stories of long ago.

Darlene (Stewart) Kingi has written and had numerous articles published, so it wasn't a matter of could she write, but from whose perspective to write.

Years ago, she had thought of writing a book mainly for her children to learn about their grandparents' lives and their work amongst the aborigines. She had returned to Cundeelee as a missionary and there had met (yes, in the outback of Australia) and married Bob Kingi, an itinerant Maori evangelist.

During these precious weeks of sharing together, we realized Darlene had been endeavoring to integrate three completely different histories or "books" into one. There was our parents' story she wanted to share, events that took place at Cundeelee, which revolved around the aboriginal people, and last but far from least, Darlene's own extremely fascinating biography.

It was because of the affinity of mine with the aboriginal culture that at the end of my stay we decided I would write this second book as well. Darlene graciously gathered up her notes and other accumulated documents and gave them to me with her blessing to use in any way I saw fit.

The Western Australian aboriginal Spinifex tribes are short on written and/or recorded true stories of their "recent" past or events in individual's lives about their struggles and triumphs - especially dealing with two cultures.

On this recent trip, I was surprised at how many of this tribe, even having known and retained friendship with our family, still requested I not take their photo. While they reminded me to give their warmest regards to my sister, brother, and mother they said "please no photos" and I honored their request. Some of the younger ones wanted to see each and every photo I had - even of loved ones who had passed on. This was a new development from when I was there in 1993.

To my aboriginal friends -
You said:
    "When you write, please only use English names of
    the aborigines;
    Whisper the name in our ears; and
    Please - no names."

On this latest trip, I was at first surprised to hear you use the word "Kunmanu" (a word meaning no name) instead of using the person's English first name, and then saying the individual's last name. When you called me and did not use my first name, you said "Kunmanu Stewart."

It was then I came to realize that some of you are caught between your traditional culture and a developing one. Now even English first names are also not to be said for a while after the death of someone who had the same first name. It is hard for me to write of my friends' lives, to satisfy everyone's request, and yet not to offend anyone while sharing their stories.

Evidence of the last fifty years indicates that future generations will want to learn of their people by name. In 1992 when you talked to my older brother Dale, you asked him about your parents. You wanted to see photos and to hear stories about them. Nevertheless, to this day you are fearful of having your pictures taken.

In this book, I will use only an aboriginal's English name so that when these stories are read, a name can be whispered. At no time in this book will I divulge any "spirit" or aboriginal given name during the telling of your story.

Still today in this culture, many are ruled by intense fear and spirit worship. This society has a mindset instilled from birth, which drives, controls, and rules every part of their lives. There is usually a great deal of fear triggered when a "spirit or soul" name of a deceased person is spoken aloud. It is simply NOT to be done. It is a HUGE taboo. Some will never reveal their aboriginal "spirit" name so that after death no one can curse them, or offend the spirits of the land.

An early study of Western Desert aboriginal languages estimated that Wangkatha consisted of approximately three thousand words. Meanings were often conveyed more by body language and drawings created in the dirt, rather than by involved details and long-winded speeches. If told in the aboriginal way with a few choice words and appropriate hand movements, many of the following stories could be told in just minutes. However, the English speaking reader without the benefit of this cultural insight would find the story difficult to follow.

It is with great care that I share the following true stories, for they have all been "gifted" to me. I have taken the liberty to set the background and stage according to the culture and knowledge I have been given. While every word is not verbatim, it is close enough to what was going on not to be a distortion of the truth. Each of these events was told to me with variations depending on the person's involvement.

We spoke of them in our home and later Dad shared parts of the information in churches we visited. A few of my parents' colleagues shared their versions with me. Aboriginal friends, my sister and brothers helped to fill in the remaining blanks.

No two people will put the same connotation on an event or see it from exactly the same perspective. If I have not told one of the following stories from your point of view, share your version with your friends and all will be richer because of it.

Words from others swirl towards me.
The decisions they made;
The consequences they dealt with;
And the lives they lived;
Make me consider my own and yes, all of our daily choices, which include the daily options of whether to whine or to shine.

But thanks to God, who always leads us in triumphal procession in Christ and through us spreads everywhere the fragrance of the knowledge of him; for we are to God the aroma of Christ among those who are being saved and those who are perishing. To the one we are the smell of death; to the other, the fragrance of life. And who is equal to such a task? 2Corinthians 2: 14 – 16 (NIV)

Read of a primitive culture, language and a race –
Exciting adventures and hardships keep pace –
Varying opinions regarding the color of a face –
Of God's love, mercy, and overwhelming Grace.

Marilyn Stewart

Wangkatha/Wangkatja = a dialect
Wangkai = the aborigines
Spinifex tribes = numerous clans of aborigines, who lived in
the inland desert area of Western Australia,
often referred to as spinifex country.

At first glance I see color,
And that you're not of my race -
I am afraid,
For I don't recognize your face -
I can flee from you,
At a very swift pace -
Or take a breath,
And for the worst I can brace -
Only to find instead of hostility,
Like a spray of mace -
A wealth of similarities -
A fascinating culture, and Grace.

Marilyn Stewart

A special note:
You will notice that at the end of each chapter are
author's notes. Please do *not* overlook them. As we proceed
through the book, they will add information by explaining
situations and the events of that chapter more fully.

Beginnings & Betrothal

Boy meets girl,
Life becomes a whirl.

They both had such ordinary beginnings - born in the early 1900's, into poor but working class homes, and in the United States of America.

The state was Washington, the city Seattle, and the year was Nineteen Hundred and Eighteen when Robert Stanley was born into the Stewart family.

Looking to give their children more opportunities and hoping to make "their fortune," they moved from Wenatchee to the big city of Seattle just before Bob was born. Here Glen Earl found even more people in desperate need of his services as a shoemaker but without the ability to pay for customized footwear. Never one to refuse to help someone in need he would accept their promise to pay after they had found work. In the Great Depression of the 1930's there was little work for the healthiest of men – and none at all for any man unable to walk.

Not only had WW1 left many maimed, so too had Infantile Paralysis (Polio). Survivors from both horrors might have escaped death but many were left crippled in body and spirit. Many men had to be carried into the shop for their first fitting, and they were terribly embarrassed to let anyone see their deformity. Few clients could afford to pay for the hides he bought from the abattoirs and tanned in the back room, let alone for the days of labor, it took to create each work of art.

He was a man ahead of his time, for he made orthopedic boots. Grown men were known to cry with joy over finally being able to stand and walk, for it meant they could now hold their head high and leave their homes to find work.

Glen Earl worked long and hard, but so did his wife Ada. Their backyard was dotted with fruit trees such as

1

plum, cherry, pear and crabapple, which the family picked as it ripened. In later years she spent many long hot days in a tiny kitchen surrounded by daughters and daughter-in-laws peeling, coring, cooking and bottling the fruit. A goat provided the family with milk and the children's breakfast "to grow by" consisted of rolled oats.

Sundays would find their family of seven warming a pew in the local Methodist Church.

Robert, or Bob as he was known in high school, excelled in Math and Science, but was almost failing in classes such as English composition and Literature - anything to do with the ability to write or spell. He also steered clear of subjects such as debate or public speaking in which he would be noticed, or those where speaking up was required for he was an extremely shy young man, due in part to his stammer. He did however excel in sports and was especially skilled in the art of boxing.

His parents were thrilled, and so very proud of Bob, when a prestigious college back East offered him a full scholarship in mechanical engineering based on his impressive test scores in math and science.

The girl was born in the state of Michigan, city of Flint, in the year Nineteen Hundred and Twenty, on her sister Doris' second birthday, to Frank and Bessie Hollinger. Ethel Frances was the second to last child born of their union and the youngest daughter in a family of four boys and four girls. Hearing of better work opportunities out West, the Hollingers moved to Seattle, but before they were able to leave, diphtheria swept through the area taking the lives of two of the girls.

At a young age, Ethel began learning to endure hardships. Ethel's baby brother Jim was two and she was only six when their Mother passed away.

Just as her father, Frank was retreating from life since the loss of his beloved wife, so too was Ethel - only no one noticed. Her father and older brothers spent long hours at work and on arriving home would sink into their favorite spots. They expected the girls to do for them what their Mother had - be it laundry or meals.

Ethel continued to fall behind in her school assignments. The teachers thought she often seemed confused, but it was not until one of them decided to seat her in the very front row for a few days that things changed. She was sent to see the school nurse. A scared Ethel took a note home to her father who read, "Get this child to a doctor and have her hearing checked."

She began a regiment of riding alone by bus into Seattle three times a week to see the ear/nose/throat specialist. She felt guilty at needing to spend her father's hard-earned money when there was no improvement. After the doctor began taking an interest in other parts of her anatomy, she refused to return. Ethel was only nine and was quite deaf; as both of her eardrums were badly damaged.

The highlight of Ethel's week had always been Sunday morning. She lived just down the street from Hillcrest Presbyterian Church on 35th Avenue, and when the bell rang, she wasted no time getting to church. Mrs. Christensen, the minister's mother, known to all as "Aunt Hannah," told the best stories. She had wonderful flannelgraph backgrounds and all of the figures for each Bible story.

Sunday school was always exciting. Even the boys sat spellbound. Ethel did not worry if she did not catch every word Aunt Hannah spoke, for she was able to follow the pictures being put up on the flannelgraph board. One morning it was again about Jesus knocking on your heart's door. She understood enough to ask Jesus into her heart. She would forever remember that day.

In order to compensate for her lack of friends due to her hearing problems, she often retreated into the pages of a book. Her favorite was the huge old family Bible that had been her mother's. Ethel took increasing comfort in reading the sacred words her mother must have read.

Education was not considered to be of great value to women as they were expected to marry and raise a family.

Her dad decided Ethel would be the one to stay home and tend the family's need, reasoning he'd be spared the expense of hiring a housekeeper. They'd not only save money with one less in school, but Ethel would not be faced with the daily reminder of her hearing loss. While it was true school was a struggle, Ethel desperately wanted to learn, to make friends, and to enjoy a "normal" life. If that was not to be, she could at least keep an eye on her younger brother Jim.

And so Ethel's formal education suddenly ended. Now she was expected to fulfill the duties of "mother" for the entire family. Another blow to the family came with the tragic drowning of her oldest brother, Frank, whom she adored.

The years passed and Ethel matured into a lovely young lady, in spirit as well as in physical beauty, attracting the attention of many eligible young men.

(We do not know how they actually met, but with both families attending the same high school we assume this was the connection.)

On Bob and Ethel's first date, he invited her to go ice-skating with him, whereupon she reluctantly informed him that she had never even been to an ice-skating rink. (She was a confident roller-skater.) The story goes that Bob thought that was just fine, and so was able to spend the evening "holding her close so she wouldn't fall" – something otherwise frowned on and thought daring for a first date.

Bob was twenty, Ethel was seventeen when on June 10 Nineteen Hundred and Thirty Eight they said their "I do's" in front of friends and family. They never thought much about it being in the sight of God.

Ethel spent all day cleaning as their evening wedding was to be held in her home. That night when they left for their honeymoon in Eastern Washington, they were chased by both sets of brothers as far as Snoqualmie Pass.

While their friends were happy for them, members of their respective families had other concerns. Bob's family was still disappointed over his decision to turn down (throw away) his golden opportunity.

Ethel's family was more concerned that they would be without a housekeeper. Her father began to think about remarriage for the first time since the death of his wife.

Family relationships were often strained on both sides as the newlyweds struggled not to take criticism personally, but to support each other regardless of their families' differing expectations.

Having felt the pain of moving away from her own family home, Bob's mother wanted nothing more than to have all of her children near her. She loved having them close and sharing daily in their lives.

A year later a bundle of joy arrived in their home. She was named Darlene Frances. Two years later, they were pleased to be expanding their family once again.

The day Robert Dale was born would turn out to be a red-letter-day in the history of the Stewart family.

- Ada Stewart underwent abdominal surgery, and hemorrhaged;
- Ethel sustained a post-partum hemorrhage, and was given 2 hours to live as a blood donor couldn't be found;
- The doctors doubted whether mother or baby would survive;
- At the end of the day in which Bob worked 16 hours to keep himself focused on something other than his fears for the two women he loved, Bob made a life changing agreement with God: "You spare my wife and my mother and I'll live for you (God) for the rest of my life."
- Robert Dale was born alive and well.
- Blood donors were found for his wife and mother.

He realized that his prayer had been answered with the safe arrival of a healthy baby and the recovery of both his wife and his mother. He remembered his promise, yet his mind continually wrestled over how he could fulfill it.

Bob was a "good man, upright morally, a loving husband" who struggled with the fact that according to the Bible these good qualities would not get him into Heaven. In recent years, he had rarely attended church. He had never read or studied the Bible before and the promise he had made to God seemed to hang over his head. He longed for peace of mind as he searched for the truth regarding God.

Bob was well aware he had a hard core of anger in him. He often worked through it by sparring or boxing – especially with his work mates. His wife and family had already learned that there were times they needed to tread lightly in his presence. He loved to dance at the club where his younger brother rocked the place with his skillful playing of a Hawaiian electric guitar.

Bob started attending the Presbyterian Church with Ethel where the Scriptures were being taught - starting with "Ye must be born again." Several years before Ethel had recommitted her life to God and ever since been praying for her beloved husband's salvation.

One day as he was reading from the Gospel of John in the Bible, Bob was struck by the fact that God really loved him. God loved him so very much that He had sent His Son Jesus (God in human form) to die for his sins and that eternal life was a free gift if he would only accept it.

Bob's pride in his good works melted as he humbly knelt in submission before the Creator of the universe asking forgiveness for his sins and committing his future into the hands of Almighty God.

His choice in accepting Jesus as his Savior and Lord radically changed not only his thinking but also his lifestyle. Over time his excuses of "but I – am too shy, don't know anything, am not qualified" changed to reflect not himself and his insecurities, but that God said His strength is manifested/shown through our weakness.

Before long, Bob and Ethel were put in charge of the church youth group. Each Sunday Bob was peppered with questions. This forced him to search the scriptures during the week to see what the Bible taught.

During the next months and years, even others began noticing a change in their values. Instead of settling down to happily living the "American dream" of a mortgage, four kids, and a dog, they had started thinking deep scary-to-dwell-on thoughts.

Could there really be a specific reason they had been born? Did God truly have a special plan and design for their lives other than what they were already living?

How did one go about finding it, and would it be right for both of them?

For a long time these questions would remain unanswered.

The Bob Ethel had married had been a quiet fellow. However, after accepting God's free gift he started sharing this good news with others on a one on one basis. Bob now had a passion to talk to people about eternity. Were they ready to face God - the creator of the heavens and the beauty all around them? Did they know God loved them?

Meantime his work mates, including his wife's father and brothers, had no time for Christians. Mr. Hollinger had put in a good word so his son-in-law could work at the mill, and that had been fine until Bob committed his life to Christ. Bob's new relatives now had a problem for they figured God had been unfair to take their much loved and needed wife and mother. As time passed, they chose to retain their anger at God over this injustice. Their resentment at God colored their outlook on life.

Bob could handle verbal abuse aimed at him, but he really got upset when they swore using God's name and ridiculed the Bible. He began to see that many statements from his work mates were just thinly veiled questions and started searching the Scriptures for answers.

On Saturday nights, Bob attended Youth For Christ meetings taking along as many young people as his car could hold.

Bob was never one for the limelight. He was like Andrew in the Bible, who brought the boy with the loaves and fishes to where he would meet the master. While Bob

7

was out "doing" and "bringing" Ethel was at home. She was doing what no one but God saw, which was encouraging, supporting, and praying for her children and husband to grow into the people they were designed to become. Ethel was developing into a faithful prayer warrior. Three years passed before their third baby, Marilyn Thelma, arrived safely. Yes, it was I, the author.

Bob was encouraged and strengthened to live a godly life by a Christian work mate named Frank Savage. Everyone, not only due to his size and work ethics but also for his integrity, respected him. Frank in turn introduced Bob to Norm Hutchinson who would later become the pastor of Arbor Heights Community Church. As Bob's friendship with Norm grew so did his appreciation of Norm's knowledge of the word of God.

Bob had a good job at Elliot Bay Mill Company, and three young children, yet his now pastor and friend Norm continued to encourage him to go to Bible School, and not just to any, but to the one way up in cold Alberta, Canada. (In those days it was considered very far from home indeed!) Learning that Norm had studied at Prairie Bible Institute in Alberta, Canada he took courage and applied to the same school.

They had been forced to wait for confirmation of a rental accommodation that would be suitable for a family. Large dormitories had been built, but only to accommodate single students. There was no student housing available on campus for a married couple, let alone for a family, so the school had to locate a place in town for them to rent.

Bible School started September 15; however, it wasn't until the 25th that the Stewart family heard "come on up suitable housing has been found."

From the human point of view, recently having purchased and moved into a new home, they finally had everything going for them.

In 1946, at the age of twenty-eight, Bob quit his good paying job, packed up his wife and three kids, their few possessions, and said their first ever goodbye to family and friends.

The congregation of the small church rallied around this young couple. The ladies helped out in ways known to them from meals to moral support, while the men using a 1936 ford axle, built a small trailer to be towed behind the Stewart's 1934 Chrysler sedan.

With their home rented out to pastor, Norm and wife Janet, they loaded the small trailer with just the basics needed to set up a home, and started out.

Little did they dream their lives would never be the same, for they had embarked on an adventure of undreamed of proportions! Bob and Ethel were much like Abraham and Sarah of the Old Testament. They were taking a step of faith and going out not fully understanding the where or why, but following the leading of The Most High God, Creator of Heaven, Earth, the Sea and yes, you and me.

Author's notes:

In my book Child of the Outback, I mentioned living for a time with a family by the name of Edstrom. It was only when I was writing this book and talking with Father Ed that I learned they had attended Arbor Heights for years. They had known my parents at the start of their "amazing journey" and Linda and I had been in the nursery together. Two of our families' long time and faithful prayer warriors were Father Ed and Hazel! Thank you!

The choice of starting a journey truly does commence with planning, stepping out, and counting the cost. It is the keeping on and the faith built during small trials that fit one for enduring the hard times. Choices, (even doing nothing is a choice) bear consequences. The first cost of their choice was hard, but not impossible to deal with. It involved leaving and being separated for a time, from their beloved family members and close-knit church friends.

The first separation from friends and family was only as far away as Three Hills, Alberta, Canada is from Seattle, Washington – roughly a thousand miles.

In the late 1940's Canada was definitely a foreign country in which Bob and Ethel were the aliens. The first step helped prepare them, a tiny bit, for the next step of faith – which would be in another foreign land and this time having no way to be able to "drive" home if they wished.

In years to come, they would daily feel the heartbreak of being over 10,000 miles from their teenage children for years at a time.

I know the song "Does Jesus Care?" often haunted their thoughts.

The fourth verse begins – "Does Jesus care when I've said "goodbye to the dearest on earth to me" and the chorus replies, "Oh yes, He cares, I know He cares, His heart is touched with my grief."

The reason I know they were often homesick is because I remember hearing Mum humming this tune, and it was only later in my teen years when I was in boarding school that I learned the name and words to the song.

Canada & Confirmation

**He said - Alaska is where I want to be,
She said - Japan is just the place for me.**

It was fall and the weather was brisk by the time they set out on their 1000-mile journey.

Traveling from Seattle to Three Hills was not simple, swift, nor uneventful. Unrecognized by them at the time, this trip actually began to lay the groundwork for Bob and Ethel's developing faith. It would prove to be a graphic representation of their lives. In the coming weeks, they would begin to learn new lessons in trust, obedience, and perseverance preparing them for the tough job God had in store for them. Growth of any significance never starts in the limelight, but in dark and often hard places where no one else sees what is happening.

It was 1946 when the Stewart family took their first tiny steps into their life-changing adventure. It began by simply heading east and then northward towards an unknown country and destiny. Everything needed to set up house-keeping had been loaded onto a trailer, covered and roped securely in place.

There were no super highways, but the maps did show the roads were paved. Having traveled to eastern Washington on their honeymoon eight years previously, Bob was thankful that he was familiar with at least a little of their journey. He had forgotten how narrow and winding these two lane roads were, and had not thought much about how the drag of the trailer would slow their travel time.

The children, having rarely traveled far by car, soon became restless. Watching the sights turned into singing, napping, and asking, "Are we there yet?" Eventually the excitement and continual motion also resulted in them becoming carsick.

They traveled from Seattle to Spokane where they spent a night with relatives on a farm. The adults talked late into the night. Nevertheless, the next morning Bob rose early, eager to be on the road. Ethel and the children on the other hand, having been sick, were not quite so eager. Bob even helped with the chores, but it had not sped up either his family or the hour of breakfast.

The trip thus far had been without incident, but Bob was chaffing and concerned over the slowness of their journey. He was only somewhat relieved once they were again on the road and finally head north.

Neither Bob nor Ethel had realized how mountainous the roads would be, nor that towing a small but extremely overloaded trailer would keep Bob from his usual "pedal to the metal" city-type of driving.

The children were busy talking and poking, singing and sightseeing until a sharp intake of breath from Bob had them on full alert. Instantly everyone became silent, straining to be first to figure out what was wrong.

The engine of the car sounded funny.

Bob eased the car off to the side of the road, lifted the hood and began checking the engine compartment. Ethel had already started to pray. Soon Bob walked back, stuck his head in the window and announced that the fuel pump had burst and he would have to get a new one. It was one of the few emergencies, for which he had not come prepared.

Things were quiet for a while. Well, as quiet as a trip can be with three children to keep track of near a roadway. Darlene and Dale vied with each other to see who would be the first to hear or see a vehicle coming in their direction. It actually was not too long a wait - maybe a half-hour until Bob was able to hitch a ride into a tiny town about seven miles further ahead.

The fellow who picked him up was not at all encouraging, but dropped him off at the only place in town that had any hope of fulfilling his need - the combination garage and filling station. Prayers were answered abundantly, for Bob "found" the exact make and model of fuel pump needed to fit the twelve-year old 1934 sedan! The fact that they had two of them surprised everyone; however, money being tight, Bob bought only one.

Bob hitched a ride back and set to work with a thankful heart. In the process of replacing the fuel pump, the screwdriver slipped creating a gaping hole in the new diaphragm. He was stunned and overcome with feelings bordering on despair.

Dale remembers Dad telling us how he had asked the Lord, "Why me? I need your help here to get my family to where we believe you have told us to go!"

Dad added that later the answer became apparent when he had hitched a ride back to town for the second and last of their inventory. The man who gave him the lift this time had many questions about God. So it was that Dad was given an opportunity to share the good news of God's unconditional love with him. Dad admitted to us that he wished the Lord had sent him the first time! Dad guessed it was not only a lesson for him in learning to trust God, but also that he not be so impatient to get a job done.

When he had turned the car northward at Coeur d' Alene and headed for the Idaho/B.C. crossing at Eastport/Kingsgate, Bob had a goal fixed in his mind. He pushed on relentlessly in order to cross the border before nightfall.

Darlene remembers the next event with cold clarity.

Finally, the border was in sight. The car in front of us was checked and cleared to go through. The gate rose and lowered. Then, as we sat waiting in the idling car, we watched in disbelief as the border patrol inspectors walked to their cars, got in, and drove away.

Had they gone for dinner? Unbeknown to Bob and Ethel, closing time at the Canadian border was 5:00 P.M., sharp. No exceptions! Not even a family with three young children ill clothed for the plummeting temperature swayed them. The border was closed until morning.

We spent the night in the car, facing the border, close to a busy railroad crossing, in below-freezing weather. Every so often Dad would turn on the engine attempting to take the deep chill out of the car's interior. It was an extremely long and incredibly cold night.

In the morning after we had been processed through customs and immigration, we stopped in the township of Yahk. There a farmer, a complete stranger, invited us into his home for a warm breakfast before we continued on our way.

To Bob and Ethel he was an angel of mercy, compassion, and encouragement. Later they would recall the words from the scripture verse in Matthew 25:40 KJV that says, "Inasmuch as ye have done it unto one of the least of these my brethren, ye have done it unto me."

They were once more on the move, but despite it being a sunny day, the air retained a nip and the wind was cold.

Bob did not mention it to Ethel, but as each hour and day passed, he was becoming quite concerned. Not only was it becoming much colder, but also the clouds looked as if they were heavily laden with snow. Watching them build added to his worry-box for it appeared they were headed straight into that menacing mass. Bob had rarely driven in snow and never in a full-blown blizzard.

Throughout the day, it crossed Bob's mind several times to wonder why God had not chosen to allow them to have smooth sailing. They could have reached their destination except for these unforeseen obstacles/trials. God certainly knew he was not a good student and he was already two weeks behind in class work. He was not looking forward to catching up. But that was just one of the many things weighing on his mind.

The children woke from a nap to see enormous snowflakes floating down and sticking to the windshield. While they shouted and clapped, Bob's stomach knotted tighter and his knuckles whitened. The roads were bad enough, being two-way and narrow. Now as well as being winding, mountainous and totally unknown, they were snowy.

Ethel closed her eyes and wished there was something she could do to help. She had never needed to learn to drive, and now was definitely no time to learn. She could at least pray. Bob had been encouraged knowing his 25 year old wife was praying, but now he needed concrete help.

The wipers were not working - they would not move at all. Bob had forgotten they were vacuum operated so almost worthless at high altitude and even more so when the engine was straining for power. The wipers had worked fine in Seattle; he was sure they weren't frozen. They were miles from a town, and just had to keep going, but how could they?

They'd have to find a solution or pull over and park. Recalling the icy conditions of the previous night spurred him to rack his brain searching for any possible innovation.

Bob briefly reflected that if he had taken the advice of his family back in Seattle, they would all be safe and snug at home right now. If he were by himself it would not be so troubling, but he had his wife and three children to consider. Both Ethel and Bob were silent, yet at the same time desperately praying for God's intervention and protection. He refocused his thoughts on their looming crisis.

"Rope! Yes, that will work! Thank you, Father. Now, where did I put that spare piece?" He came to a stop in a tight, but adequate pull off. Bob located the rope and gently eased the wipers from the grip of the icy windshield. The extra rope was just long enough to feed through each front wing window after making a loop around each wiper.

Nervously huddled together under all the pillows and extra blankets the kids tried to stay quiet and keep warm. Bob and Ethel took turns pulling on the rope ends, which in turn moved the wipers to clear the windows of snow. They were moving once again, but it was frightfully cold.

They were learning and now living the words of a song they had sung in church. "Day by day and with each passing moment, strength I find to meet my trials here, trusting in my Father's wise bestowment, I've no cause for worry or for fear...."

Suddenly Bob tensed. Rounding a bend in the road, he saw a row of red taillights. Trucks finding it too hard to stay on the road were pulling over at any wide spot they could find in order to save their vehicles and cargo. He watched in dismay as a car ahead slid slowly off the road and into the ditch. Bob, who would normally have stopped to help, instead found it was all he could do to keep the car and trailer from joining it. He had to keep on going.

Throughout the night, he watched helplessly as one vehicle after another began to slide and slither until it drifted relentlessly off the road and into the grasp of a powdery bank of snow. In between gusts of swirling snow, Bob had been thankful to be able to catch intermittent glimpses of several red taillights ahead.

Black ice - nasty stuff he could not see and visible slick icy patches Bob dreaded became even more frequent. The blowing snow made it difficult to see. The speed, though steady, continued at a snail like pace. Bob, as much as was possible, had known where it was safe to drive, for he had been following the tracks left in the snow by the vehicles ahead. Every so often, he had caught a reassuring glimpse of a large truck at the front of the pack. Its weight and wide tires were doing a good job of carving out a path in the snow for all to follow.

After hours of slowly creeping ever onward and upward, Bob realized he was finally right behind the truck. The driver began honking, then put his arm out of the window motioning as if he wanted Bob to pass. Not having seen any cars coming from the other direction for over an hour, Bob risked steering over into the wrong lane.

As he drove up beside the truck, Ethel rolled down her window and they heard the driver holler, "I can't see! I've been watching you in my mirrors and you have the best headlights – you take the lead and we'll all follow you." Bob knew his car had sealed beams, but oh, how he would rather follow in the safe, wide, pre-made tracks, than lead any day. [How like life – for he was not a natural leader.]

His thoughts were quick and fleeting; "Oh, God what more do you have in store for us?" at the same time he hollered back "Okay." Cautiously he inched passed the truck and returned once more into the correct lane.

Once again, Bob pulled the rope and the wiper cleared a swath. Ethel pulled it back and they peered through the windshield trying desperately to see where they were going. The children were also spotters - for cars to avoid yes, but their main job was to watch for the edge of the road. Bob could no longer see which lane he was driving in as the dividing line was no longer visible. Darlene and Dale each took a side to monitor, and all prayed except Marilyn, who being only two slept on.

While the car and overloaded trailer continued to climb higher up Crowsnest Pass, the heavily laden truck fell ever further behind. A few cars tucked in tight on the trailer's bumper in order to make use of the car's bright headlights. The winds were fierce, blowing snow into drifts and swirling the flakes in ever changing directions. It was hard to see out the icy windshield.

Neither Bob nor Ethel wanted to be the first to admit to what they thought they were seeing reflecting off of the frosty car hood for fear they were just imagining the faint glimmer of lights. Ah, kids – "Lights, I see lights" was suddenly screeched from the back seat! Marilyn awoke with a start to catch her breath in alarm, while the others' breathing finally returned to normal.

They had crested the Pass and were headed for the town of Cowley. Then disaster struck once more. Hearing a dragging sound and feeling a tug on the wheel Bob eased off of the throttle and was greatly relieved when he found a safe spot in which to pull off and park. A quick inspection showed that an essential part of the trailer hitch had broken.

A short discussion with Ethel led to Bob's unhitching the trailer. They would just have to leave it there and trust God to keep their stuff safe from vandals. He would take his family to their destination and come back as soon as he could. After unhitching the trailer they said a heartfelt prayer of thanksgiving for safe travel over the mountain, before once again resuming their journey.

Traveling was much easier and faster without the heavy trailer wagging like an unruly tail.

Bob had so hoped to make it to Three Hills by nightfall, but they were only as far as Fort Macleod and he was totally exhausted so decided to get a good night's rest. He started checking for a warm place out of the storm where his family could spend the night.

Darlene remembers Dad began looking for a hotel/motel or anywhere his family could get some much-needed sleep. The only rooms available in these "hotels" were located right over the bars. When they heard there were children in the car, first one and then another refused him accommodations.

Dad learned that the policy of these establishments, created for the distinct purpose of resting weary bones, was to allow neither children nor animals in any of their rooms.

After being rejected at each place, our desperate and exhausted father had some very strong words with the management of the last hotel in town. For a price the manager finally agreed to allow us to stay, on the condition that no one heard or saw a child in the building.

We were smuggled up the back stairs and our family left very early in the morning as agreed, but not before "coughing up" an added tariff.

And so the Stewart family was once again headed towards Three Hills and P.B.I. After all the mountains they had come through no one could believe the vastness of the prairies. Where were the three hills? On the northern horizon were three faint contours, and from those the township had gained its name.

Upon arrival, Bob quickly registered as a student, found out where they would be staying and briefly outlined their adventures. Bob needed to go back and retrieve the trailer, but first he had to get his family settled. A widow, with grown children, had agreed to share her home with this alien couple and their children until they had retrieved their belongings and could set up house.

Bob was overwhelmed and grateful when he learned that Mr. Mumford, one of the teachers, had determined to make the drive with him. The wind howled and the snow flurries continued falling as Bob and Mr. Mumford – a humble, gracious, kind-hearted man, headed back to fetch and repair the trailer. They left without sleeping for time was crucial, the weather was steadily worsening, and Bob was fretting about his trailer and its essential contents.

What a trip! Bob would never forget the blizzard they endured, the relief at finding the trailer untouched, or the ease of completing the repairs. At one point on the return journey overcome by tiredness coupled with the whiteout conditions, both driver and passenger fell asleep.

For how long they slept, neither one knew.

Both were thankful for God's amazing protection. Their fellowship would knit them together as life-long friends. As Bob witnessed Mr. Mumford's peace and serenity during many long stress filled hours his trust in the Lord's care took a gigantic leap.

Bob and Ethel had gone from living in a brand new three-bedroom home with all of the amenities, to renting a tiny two-bedroom dwelling. Now they needed not only to carry their water from the neighbor's house, but also to use a long–drop toilet located outside at quite a distance.

Although they had come from wet and cold Seattle, they were shocked by the frigid intense cold where –25 degrees F was not unusual for a winter day.

Bob had not thought a lot about what it would entail to return to school. He did not expect to breeze through his classes, but had never considered how much thinking and writing would be required - daily. He sometimes wondered what he had been thinking, for spelling and grammar had been his worst subjects!

He could not have imagined that by going to Bible school he would set himself up to take a spelling test every week! Not only that, but would learn to read a map, memorize five verses a week, take music theory, be assigned to a singing teacher and even learn to conduct a song. He had been out of school for a long time, and sometimes he even wondered if maybe it had been too long. He would be required not only to write three five thousand-word papers, but also to make a twelve foot by three-foot chart depicting Daniel's vision.

At times, he wondered what some of these classes had to do with increasing his knowledge of the Word of God. As he talked with other students, he was reminded that the school majored in Bible and missions and one never knew where one might end up or what skill might be needed.

It was often late into the night that the light burned over the kitchen table where Bob and Ethel read and discussed his homework. Students' wives with children were not expected to attend classes full time, but they were encouraged to take at least a few of the courses offered. They were also informed they were welcome to support, assist, or help their husbands – not do their homework mind – but aid them by discussing and clarifying the questions and concepts listed on their assignments.

Bob and Ethel drank in the teaching and Bible classes. They also made heart connections and forever friendships with other freshmen.

Spring arrived and Bob decided to seek employment for the summer back in the USA. Before he left he wanted to have his family snug in its own little place. Bob had found a tiny house in Three Hills, but it would need to be moved to Ruarkville. The weekend to move was set. The day arrived cloudless and full of promise.

The move began. Instead of using horses as they had planned, a tractor was needed for the ground was beginning to thaw faster than they had expected. In fact, they hooked up four tractors – two red Massey Fergussons, a John Deere and one other. Having been placed onto skids the house moved slowly in the wake of the tractors.

All went well until they reached the final bend. Unexpectedly, just 100 yards from its destination the last tractor lost traction and in correcting, broke through into the notorious gumbo. Soon all of the tractors were straining, mud was flying and the house, settling ever deeper, became "stuck in the mud" in the very center of the road.

After much discussion, the men decided the house would just have to stay there until the mud hardened. The tractors and men were needed in their fields for planting time had arrived. Alberta has a very short growing season and every day counted against them. They would not waste their precious time moving a house that did not want to budge.

It was a summer neither Bob nor Ethel ever forgot. They were young – still in their twenties - and were being taught crucial life lessons to trust God in the everyday things as well as in regards to their future.

Ethel was stuck living in a house in the middle of the road, without her husband to call on, with three children, no electricity, running water, or a bathroom. It was humiliating to live in a house that sat blocking an entire road.

It was dusty and dirty, uncomfortable and lonely. Some days she wondered at the hardships she and her children were enduring.

A grader made a road around their home giving access to Ruarkville. Ethel and the children had to walk to their nearest neighbor to use their restroom and to get water. All summer they were the joke of the community. However, come fall when the mud was hard enough everyone pitched in to get the house in place before the snows arrived.

Ethel had a completely new appreciation for all of the comforts of home – even the distant outhouse was a blessing.

Regarding that summer, Bob's memories were totally different, but just as vivid. He found work as a second mate on a tugboat and experienced his own time of growth. He had rarely done a dish in his life and had never cooked. Now his job included taking his turn as the chief cook and bottle washer. He learned to make porridge, scrub pots, and traverse a log boom. His run was from the San Juan Islands down to Seattle and he learned fast that no one had just one job. He was expected to take his turn at keeping the logs floating and to make sure that no blockage occurred.

The first couple of times Bob ran the logs his supposed "mates" allowed him to almost be killed as a sort of "initiation test" to check the caliber of this preacher man. Seeing Bob was a disaster waiting to happen, one crewmember showed Bob a couple of tricks he could practice in order to stay on and not under the rolling logs.

When a jam up did occur, it required that Bob leave the safety of the boat. It was a frightening experience to step, and then run from log to log, as they bobbed up and down tossing violently in and out of the water. He learned to move carefully, but quickly in order to keep his footing while he jabbed and prodded at the stacked timbers. The job entailed making sure each log floated freely.

Each time he was out there pitching and swaying, he was also hoping and praying desperately that he not fall between the logs. The times Bob did fall into the cold water he was all too well aware that death was very near as the rough water caused the unruly logs to strike sharply one against the other. They all feared this task, and some ran the logs in desperation to get it over, and shook for a while upon return. Soon silence replaced the sneers they had given the "preacher man." He sweated just as they did, but he had a strange peace about him.

Ethel was like a sponge soaking up information, both in the classes she was taking as well as from reading and discussing Bob's lessons with him. She forged several heart connected lifelong friends of which one of the dearest was Bernice Callaway. Ethel learned so much from the dear caring women in her Bible study group. Bible truths – such as trust, faith and praying were important as were the cares shared regarding their children. Ethel, having had one stillborn baby, empathized and mourned with her friend Bernice over the loss of her baby, Stephen.

The next two summers Bob sought employment in Three Hills in order to be near his family. He worked for a farmer named Milton Smithers and when the crops were in and he was no longer needed, he found a job driving a coal truck. Bob was required not only to drive the truck and deliver the coal, but was also obligated to shovel it into the basement coal bins. In an attempt to keep as much of the coal dust out of the house as was possible, someone had designed a trapdoor which was located outside and right above the coal bin. The housewife just needed to make sure the basement door was closed and that she didn't have laundry drying down there. Bob learned to keep his customers happy by knocking and warning the inhabitants to take precautions when he was about to dump coal into their bin.

At the time, these jobs seemed only to serve two purposes; to put food on the table, and to pay for their housing and tuition for the next year. In later years, Bob would find many of the skills and lessons learned during those years to be very useful indeed.

Three years of study and work passed rapidly. It was April 1949 the end of a school year and time once again for the weeklong missionary conference. Next year at this time he would be sitting his finals and graduating.

Over the years, Bob and Ethel had heard many speakers. Bob still thought often of the Eskimos in Alaska and Ethel of the people of Japan. Nevertheless, neither was convinced that they would end up anywhere, except back in Seattle helping in their church.

They were listening to yet another missionary speaker. Suddenly Bob's wandering mind was arrested by the slides being shown of primitive nomadic dark skinned people. He was stunned by the pull of his heartstrings towards them. Even now, he was not good at spelling or geography so when he went to the library to locate the place he had difficulty finding it. He first looked at Europe where he found Austria. When he finally located Australia, he was shaken by how far away from the USA it was; but a strange excitement kept building in his heart.

That night he opened his Bible and read the words from John 10:16 KJV, they seemed to leap off the page.

"And other sheep I have which are not of this fold, them also I must bring, and they shall hear my voice; and there shall be one fold and one shepherd." Next morning he read Psalms 2 and verse 8 gripped his very soul. "Ask of me, and I shall give thee the heathen for thine inheritance, and the uttermost parts of the earth for thy possession."

The thought of his family back in Seattle sent a shudder through him. Whatever would his Mother say? She was upset enough with them being so far from home in Canada. More to the point, what would Ethel say to yet another country to consider? Especially one they had never even heard of.

But why was he getting worried about it? Everyone knew that no missionary society accepted couples with children, and he was over thirty years of age. He continued to reason that no one would take a man the army wouldn't accept due to a heart murmur. Besides he had a deaf wife – well almost for she could hear some words and music as long as she had batteries, and remembered to use her hearing aid.

A week passed, and then another and still Bob could not shake the images he had seen, or the verses he'd read, from his mind. There was nothing else to do but confide in his wife as to what was going on in his heart. One evening Bob summoned his courage and hesitatingly told Ethel he needed to talk to her about something after the kids had gone to bed. To his surprise, Ethel responded by saying, "I need to discuss something with you also."

Being very nervous about the other's response to such an important issue, they wished to discuss, and not knowing what the other had in mind, they decided to write the information down on paper and swap. They agreed to read silently what the other had written then discuss it.

As they gingerly unfolded each other's paper neither one could believe what they were reading for they were almost identical. In amazed silence, they read the same Bible verses starting with the one in the book of John, and both said they had felt God wanted them to go work with the primitive aborigines in Australia.

They were stunned for they were two ordinary unskilled people with no resources, and both had had other desires. They agreed that though it seemed most unlikely that they'd be considered they would write a letter of inquiry to the mission board in Sydney, Australia.

Summer passed with Bob once again working for Milton Smithers. In September he started his last year of Bible training. They had heard nothing from the mission board – not a peep.

One day in early October, a large thick packet arrived bearing Australian stamps. Enclosed they found forms to fill out for each member of the family. The Australian Aboriginal Evangelical Mission was indeed very interested in them. They would need medical check-ups including chest X-rays, detailed personal and spiritual history of the parents, as well as passports and visas.

They decided to fill out the application papers even though they were sure nothing would happen, and certainly not before Bob's graduation the following spring. The doctor said Australia sounded like just the right climate for Darlene, for in his opinion, she might not live through another Canadian winter.

It was astounding - nothing was a roadblock to their going - not Bob's heart murmur, Ethel's hearing, or Darlene's health, their age, or even the fact that they had three children. They were reassured that this was the Lord's doings, for they knew of several single individuals who had been turned down having far fewer "handicaps".

In November, they heard again from the mission board and once again, the letter stated they were needed - Urgently! A mission station was about to be established in Western Australia by the missionary speaker, Albert Sopher and his wife.

Bob's practical skills and availability were of more importance to them than a diploma signifying completion of his studies. While encouraged on the one hand Bob was secretly disappointed that the credentials he had worked so hard towards would never be his.

They took all of their correspondence, doubts, questions and insecurities and laid them "on the table" before their beloved and godly principal L.E. Maxwell. He was well aware that it simply did not happen this way, and that truly God's hand had to be in it for all of the negatives to be ignored. His counsel to them was not to stay until April just for Bob to graduate, adding they should leave now as there was little snow, and to be on their way to Australia as soon as possible.

Mr. Maxwell was quite a character and knew that Bob was still very reluctant to speak in public. He had not overcome either his nervousness or self-consciousness. At a meeting in the tabernacle before they left, Mr. Maxwell came down out of the pulpit and into the pews where he grabbed a hold of Bob by his collar and the seat of his trousers. In a booming voice, he announced to everyone that he was going to hold Bob up and Bob was going to tell them all what the Lord was doing in his life and where he would be serving in the near future.

The students were saddened to learn the Stewarts would not be staying on for Bob to graduate in April, but were thrilled to hear of how the Lord was directing them to a new work overseas, which had their principal's full approval, endorsement and blessing.

Oh how they'd miss these who had been strangers - now so many were such good and precious friends.

Everything was happening so fast!

Bob was in a hurry now to get going south – down out of Canada before the snow arrived. The Thanksgiving holiday was almost upon them when they started their thousand-mile journey homeward. The long-awaited snow began gently falling as they pulled away from their tiny house in Ruarkville with all its memories.

Having made this trip several times, now Bob was much more confident and they were making good time.

They were just starting down yet another hill, when Bob felt a hard jerk on the steering wheel. He immediately slowed and started easing off the road. A movement by his window caught his eye, and looking out he saw a tire rolling down the road.

My older brother Dale recalls the incident.

Dad yanked on the hand brake, jumped out, and started running down the hill after the crazily bouncing tire. Mum started praying and eight-year-old Dale shouts at her that she is being silly for what can God do about their tire! Dale, who watched this tire bouncing so merrily down the road away from them, said the following picture is forever burned in his memory. They all watched in stunned silence, for as the words came out of Dale's mouth, the tire took another high bounce only this time to leap backwards into the ditch, fall on its side, and lay still.

Was it so incredible then that there was even a proper pull-off where Bob was able to move the vehicle to safety in order to work on the trailer's broken axle?

Unhitching the car, Dad drove to the nearest service station. The owner told him that he did not know of any place that had a 1936 axle; however, he could certainly paw through their metal scrap heap out back.

Doing, rather than sitting, was often Bob's way of handling stressful situations, and so he began digging through the conglomeration of various old parts. By now, he was busy praying as he yanked, pulled and tossed pieces aside in ever-growing frustration coupled with disappointment. Uncovering yet another section of mostly rusted, twisted, unusable metal, he paused.

The station owner looked at Bob standing in the doorway clutching a good, but very rusty old 1936 Ford axle – the exact model he had asked about – and shook his head in wonderment saying, "I can't believe it – I don't remember it being there!"

The repairs were accomplished and the turtle-like pace was resumed once again. Being back on the road and humming right along for several hours eased some of Bob's tension.

All during the trip homeward, the situation they would face when they got to Seattle and told family and friends of their plans preoccupied their minds. They had just left a missionary-minded school and culture and were returning to families who had no understanding of what was happening in their lives, or the call they felt was definitely of God.

While they were in school, they had received word that Bob's oldest brother Earl, who worked in Alaska, was missing and presumed dead. [His body was never found and for the remainder of her life, his mother alternated between mourning him and believing that someday he would walk through the door.] Bob mourned the loss of his brother and now was fretting over giving his mother more sorrow regarding their imminent departure. How would their families and friends react to their life-changing radical decision?

They had become accustomed to a tiny home in a small neighborhood, and now they were returning to Seattle and would need to sell their three-bedroom home. It had been rented out, but renting and selling a house were two different things for there was no market - people were just NOT buying homes.

Once again, they laid out their request before the Lord. "If this is definitely where you want us to go, then sell this house fast. We need the payment made in full. We also need it in cash. If you do this – which everyone says, with this market, is impossible - then with the proceeds we will buy our tickets to Australia."

They would need to pack most all of their clothing and necessary belongings into heavy metal fifty-five gallon drums and send them ahead by ship.

Bob was very good at organizing and getting things done, but knowing he would need to get up and speak (and not just in his home church) about going to another country as missionaries – that scared him to his very core.

Author's notes:

Frank Savage invited Bob to talk to his previous work mates at their noon break. He stood in the courtyard on a soapbox, as was the custom, and started to tell his story or as some said - preach. Before long, a big burly fellow came up and told him to shut up or be shut up. Bob chose to continue and the fellow punched him on the nose. Bob rubbed his nose shook his head and kept on preaching. He was dimly aware something strange had taken place. The man was mystified - stunned by Bob's unexpected behavior and after a grimace and a shrug walked away. It was only later that evening while sharing the events of the day with Ethel that they realized what was nagging at his subconscious.

It was that Bob had not immediately retaliated with a swift knockout blow of his own.

While at school they had learned a hymn that begins with the words – "What a wonderful change in my life has been wrought (taken place) since Jesus came into my heart."

They humbly praised God for they realized the difference in Bob was truly from HIM.

Beyond all doubt Bob's reactions had been changed.

It was God's love, mercy and grace for him that had changed his thinking and attitude towards life and humankind in general.

Remembering from whence he had come continued to stand him in good stead during future hard times. It gave him hope for a struggling, often warring primitive nomadic people. He could see his former self in their actions – and except for the grace of God, he too would still be in "retaliation mode" in his own actions and thinking.

Bob and Ethel Stewart   June 10, 1938

Australia & Arrival

No shops, no phones, not even any rain,
Life is excruciatingly hard on our tired brains.

In February of 1950, travel was quite different from what it is today. Missionaries heading overseas took the sea route. Although it took longer, it was in reality substantially cheaper. The Stewart family flew because the latest communication from the mission board was worded "needed urgently." The airplane was small and far less comfortable, seating just 36 passengers. Distances were charted within the fuel range of the airplane making numerous stops from North America to Australia a necessity.

The war years were not that far in the past and so, instead of travel most people were getting on with their lives. There was little thought given to a people no one knew about in far away country which was part of the British Commonwealth of Nations.

Bob and Ethel knew very little about their destination, just that they both felt a pull towards these primitive tribes of aborigines in the Western Australian Desert.

Darlene, being ten and a half, remembers the trip from a different frame of reference. Here is her introduction to Australia.

As we circled to land in Sydney on February 26, 1950, we could hardly believe our eyes for before us lay a modern city. It was complete with high-rise buildings, landscaped parks, a rail system, and even a zoo.

All we knew about Australia was what we had seen on a missionary's slides: aborigines sitting on the sandy desert. No one said anything about a city where everyone spoke with an English accent. Where was the desert? Where were the aborigines?

We recognized Mr. Telfer, the mission president, and his tiny wife from the slides. Instead of going straight to the train, the adults started talking about a hold-up of our drums. We should expect to stay in Sydney for several weeks. Someone drove us to our accommodation at a girls' hostel, but not once did we see an aboriginal. I remember all of the intensity of helping Mum pack, of getting the house sold, of saying good-bye to school friends, family and people at church, and now I hear Mr. Telfer say they have nothing for us to do for several weeks.

We had arrived in midsummer and our living space was restricted. Mum and I had our hands full keeping track of Dale and Marilyn. This enforced inactivity was frustrating for we had been told to hurry and come. Dad could have finished college. Mum was expecting another child in July – in a strange country - and I could have finished my school year in the USA. It was certainly a trying time.

When we attended church, we were shocked to find churches full of believers who could easily have been doing the task themselves. We had come halfway around the world to preach the good news of the Gospel to the aborigines of this land, only to find ourselves under a cloud of suspicion.

It seemed the need had been greatly misrepresented. Australian Christians rejected Dad and Mum's testimony of divine guidance changing their lives and bringing them here. Instead of support from fellow members of the Body of Christ, there was interrogation.

"What do you think you are going to do here?" "Why didn't you stay in America and preach to the Negroes and Indians?" "How dare you come here and make us look bad." "All that can be done is already being done." "Who told you that you were needed down here?"

At the same time, no one seemed to know of anyone who was either living or working with the aborigines. Visions of the aborigines seemed like a mirage – in the midst of modern Sydney. There was not one spear-carrying individual to be seen. Every home we entered had more of this world's goods than we had had back home.

A visit to the zoo, to Lunar Park, and a ride on a double-decker bus are memories that have lingered in

Darlene's mind for over fifty years; the sense of a great letdown has also stayed with her to this very day.

Everything was totally foreign to what Bob and Ethel had expected, yet they were still convinced they were there for the express purpose of sharing God's love with the aborigines.

Their seven drums finally arrived and Ethel gave Bob the itemized list of the contents of each. In them were essential household items including clothes and bedding to last for five years. There were family photographs, recipe books, toys, tools, and a few treasured pictures to hang.

The custom officials were thorough, and then said anything that could not be repacked and sealed into the drums had to be left. The flour sifter was bent out of shape, but still useable. Even though Bob did his best to cram everything back in the containers, many things had to be left on the dock – a customs official's bonus.

The Stewarts could now leave the city and its wealth for the west and the stone-age nomadic people of the desert.

Before they left, the board informed them, "Where you are going there is no dependable source of water." Bob and Ethel left feeling confident that if the mission board knew about a water problem they would surely have a solution in mind.

Bob and Ethel little dreamed they would send out a family with three children plus a newborn to a place one hundred fifty six miles from the nearest town, stores or doctor, with no housing, electricity or water – running or not.

Albert Sopher took Bob with him to Perth to obtain written permission from the minister of Aboriginal Affairs and to hopefully be assigned a reservation on which to work. First - they had to provide specific information.

Who were the people applying for the permit?

What did they intend to do?

Where did they anticipate working?

When would they be ready to start?

Why did they wish to work with aborigines?

How would they co-operate with the government?

He appointed them to reopen the [not long closed down one-man operation] reservation called Cundeelee. They came away rejoicing over the favorable outcome.

Bob and Albert Sopher proceeded to Cundeelee. Ethel went to Kalgoorlie and stayed with a family until her baby arrived. Darlene, Dale and Marilyn were left with a single Australian woman in Loongana. Hundreds of miles now separated the Stewart family.

Bob remembered the summer of training he'd had on the tugboat for his ability to cook and clean up was needed the first several months when he had to batch at Cundeelee.

Ethel had a week to settle into the brush-covered tent – now called home, a pit-toilet (one-holer/outhouse) a considerable distance away, no electricity or running water, and a primus (camp stove) to cook on, before her children arrived on the scene.

She thought back to the summer she had lived in the middle of the road, and saw it now in a new light. It had been preparing her for the same type of situation regarding water and electricity, and she was suddenly thankful for that awful long summer she had experienced.

It was August and winter when the Stewart's were finally reunited as a family and the older children got to see their tiny new brother – Stephen John.

Bob and Ethel were in shock on several levels – not the least of which was the weather, or lack of it. Seattle had majored in rainy days, and here even the winter days were sunny. Ethel had never experienced such dry skin, painfully bright sun, and extremely low humidity.

They were city born and used to telephones, sirens, cars, and airplanes flying over head – just the hum of city life. They had never thought of "all the comforts of home" until they did not have anything to sleep on but army cots, and a plank of wood on a tea chest, which made a table. They did have a chair and a torch (flashlight) for a light.

To Ethel, the silence not only meant no police, fire department, shops, telephone, but also no doctor. No help was instantly available for their month old baby.

There were small and annoying flies as well as the big ones called "blowies" – everywhere, as were the native people and their half-dingo (for hunting kangaroo) dogs.

Ethel wondered how her children were going to get an education - let alone a good one.

What could she do to help these aboriginal mothers when she could barely hear, did not understand their language or culture, and was having a variety of physical problems?

Author's notes:

In my first book – Child of the Outback – I tell about our thirty-six-hour crew-pause in Hawaii, the unscheduled stop in the Canton Islands, and miracle take-off.

Over the years, the three younger children alternated between correspondence (home schooling with assigned work) and a classroom situation with aborigine children. It all depended on whether or not there was a teacher at Cundeelee. As the oldest and being so much further ahead, Darlene remained on the correspondence lessons sent from Perth to children in the outback areas.

Stewart family

Rations

Second Home

Culture & Conflict

**Life was harsh, it wasn't a game,
Tjamu and Lyunku, their Wangkai names.**

At no time had Bob or Ethel taken any foreign language courses, nor had they been given any linguistics training prior to their assignment.

Neither of them realized just how spoiled they'd been - until now when they had no shops, library, church, medical facility, or even the luxury of water through turning on a tap.

Their assets were hearts full of compassion, and a will to learn to communicate with a stone-age civilization.

It had taken no time at all for the keenly observant Wangkai people to realize Ethel had a problem hearing them. Their life often depended on them catching the tiniest of movements. They were used to paying attention to everything that moved or had breath and even some things that didn't.

Eventually they would draw their own conclusions regarding something new. They didn't even have a word for our overused one word query of "WHY?" The idea of questioning Ethel regarding her hearing loss was unthinkable. It was simply accepted as an unchangeable fact.

"Why" is a question an inquiry word, and as such not needed, because a person was to observe and accept. The very idea of questioning, especially the why of something, was offensive. Time would reveal the answer. Either you would find out or you would not – so one did not worry about it. If it was within their ability and desire to change something, then that was considered essential.

Everything that would not enhance their way of life was ignored as a nonessential, not relevant, nor of any importance.

It was an undeniable fact that Ethel was deaf, period. It became an unwritten tribal custom that when an aboriginal was about to meet Ethel for the first time he/she was to be accompanied by a resident from camp. As soon as Ethel was spotted, the newcomer would be given three hardly-discernible signs. Without a word being spoken aloud, the information had now been shared as to who she was and that she was deaf. This information also clued them in to observe even more closely others' interaction with her, which they in future would copy so as not to offend her and yet at the same time not violate their own code of ethics.

Usually a "spirit or soul" name was given only after lengthy observation of the individual regarding their nature and habits. However, in Ethel's case, the name givers came to a speedy assessment and she was given an aboriginal name almost immediately. Ethel would be called "Pina Lyunku".

For a while Ethel not only had a disadvantage due to her lack of hearing, but also because she didn't have as much direct and varied a contact with the people as did her husband Bob.

Ethel did have one big advantage. She was accustomed to watching people – their facial expressions and their body language. If she could have been granted one wish for a skill to help her in this primitive society, she couldn't have chosen a better one, because most of their conversation was non-verbal and conveyed by simple and swift hand and facial movements.

It took Ethel's eyes and Bob's hearing to catch anything being said. Most of the time the people tried to get across what they were saying, but when one wished to "talk" and not be seen or heard by Bob and Ethel, the person just turned his/her back. It only took a few silent seconds to exchange a couple of gestures and the message or information had been shared.

All Bob and Ethel wanted to do was to share the good news of Jesus and His love with the aborigines and help them in any way possible. They did not want to infringe upon or change their culture and were concerned as to how best to help these primitive people – for the long term.

When one cannot communicate adequately, it is hard to learn very much, least of all, what these peoples' hopes and dreams were. It took a while to realize their lives existed in one dimension, just one day at a time. They lived in the NOW. The past they could not do anything about; there was no guarantee of a future, so only the now was relevant.

It was as simple as hunting and gathering enough food in order to stay alive for yet another day. Upon killing and cooking, a kangaroo was consumed immediately – all of it. They had no way to preserve it and whatever little remained their dogs and the flies fought over.

Another example of their ages old lifestyle at first constantly frustrated Ethel. It was over not being able to give them medicine for today and tomorrow. Whatever the amount they were given, they took right away - all of it.

One day while reading in Matthew 6 she was suddenly struck by verses 25-34. She reread the verses. While Bob and she had trouble putting into practice the "take no anxious thought" regarding food, clothes, health, - their daily needs - they would not have to teach the people about these concepts. She thought, "They are an example to us for they live the verses regarding do not worry. What we can share with them is the part that says our Heavenly Father not only knows our needs, but also cares about each of us as an individual."

Their spoken vocabulary consisted of only necessary words, which totaled about 3000. This meant most of the words Bob and Ethel took for granted simply did not exist. The following are just a few of the things that were "missing." Numbers past three, days of the week, time, the alphabet (their language was unwritten), left and right. While they understood and lived by the concept of choice and consequence, they did not have a word for either.

For the Spinifex aborigines living in isolation in the interior or outback of Australia, there had been very few new things assimilated into their society for thousands of years. The first real change to the lifestyle of the interior aborigines began when the railroads were built across areas they traveled. [The impact had been much different for the coastal aborigines who suffered devastating changes in their lifestyle as soon as the first British settlers arrived.]

There was a severe drought in the 1950's and their lives were in further jeopardy when atomic weapons testing began in their walkabout areas - where they lived, roamed, and hunted. [This will be addressed further in the chapter titled "Facts & Fiction".]

Bob was very happy working under Albert Sopher, the very man whose slides had so moved them. Albert kept the books, worked with the government, kept the mission board in Sydney informed via letters, while Bob worked willingly at whatever task he was asked to perform.

Bob was an excellent driver so he did the supply runs, a sharp shooter which brought meat to the camp, and most of the hard labor for he was bigger stronger and younger than Albert. Bob enjoyed being out in the fresh air working and interacting with the people.

It was not long before other men and women arrived to work along side the original team. The mission board would notify Cundeelee by letter or telegram advising of their arrival time. Some were visitors, others stayed for months, a few stayed for years, but all were required to have government approval to be on the reservation. None would find it easy. It was just as big a shock for the Aussies as for the North Americans. The only difference was the Australians could return home quicker and with less expense.

For two years, Bob had been able to take a back seat in regards to leadership. One day Albert Sopher confided in Bob that he could no longer cope with the responsibilities and that he and family would be leaving very shortly. Bob and Ethel had been there since the beginning, and were the only full-time/career married missionaries at Cundeelee. Albert had already written to the mission board recommending that Bob be appointed as Superintendent.

He had only been a Christian for ten years, had not finished Bible School, nor had he paid much attention to how

Albert handled the administrative duties. Albert made it his business to familiarize Bob with the requirements of the job.

From the government standpoint, Robert S. Stewart was now in charge and fully responsible for every detail imaginable. Whether it was the giving out of rations, cutting and delivering sandalwood, keeping all of the required records, all were things he had to make sure got done and were accurately written up. He had to document every detail concerning each person who came to or went from Cundeelee.

Bob was an unassuming fellow – not one for being noticed - and still had trouble with reading, spelling and grammar. Suddenly he was in charge of writing detailed reports for both the government and the mission board.

Furthermore, he had to ensure that each aboriginal had an English name - even if he had to assign it to him/her. To do that he had to know to whom they were related in order to name them according to their family group.

The government also insisted on knowing who was present in camp at any given time. The superintendent had to fill in detailed forms: who worked, who received government rations, who had gone to hospital, for what reason, and how they had traveled there, who had died and under what circumstances, and any births. He also had to record the names and occupations of all the white staff.

He soon learned he was dealing with two groups and their conflicting agendas. The government, required the information for their personal records - not to be publicized; whereas the mission board, desired details of the peoples' lives in order to inform their worldwide readers.

Bob and Ethel were in a foreign country under and representing a missionary society who barely knew them, as well as in the beginning stages of a work with a primitive tribe generally considered to be sub-human.

Many times if it had not been for the needs of the people, and the assurance they felt that they were where they were meant to be, Bob and Ethel would have packed up and said "goodbye." [*In later years, Ethel confided that had it*

*not been for the life and writings of Amy Carmichael she did
not think she could have survived their first term.*]

It would have been so much easier to live in a culture
they understood, with family and friends nearby to
encourage them when times were tough than to be aliens in a
distant country, living far from civilization, and working
with a people that most wanted to forget existed. The fact
that they were in the same situation as the aborigines tended
to knit them together. For the most part, they too were NOT
welcome in town.

Years before, Bob had started carrying a New
Testament in his shirt pocket and daily practiced sneaking a
"read" at any opportunity. Now he studied even more
diligently for he felt inadequate to the responsibility given
him. Bob and Ethel realized that regardless of how they
personally felt regarding this change in events, God had
allowed this to happen.

When the Sopher family left, Ethel sorely felt the
lack of adult female companionship in which one shares how
to fix a meal with limited amount of food and water, and no
electricity, to caring for sick children with no doctor
available. Their leaving had been a severe blow, for Alta and
Albert had been their mentors, had five children, and at that
time were the only other "white" couple at Cundeelee.

At first, the tribal people thought the Sopher family
had just gone walk-about and would return, but finally
grasped the idea of gone walk-about, finished, no more. As
understanding took hold, they began keeping a wary eye on
Bob to see if he would change now that he was "boss."

Before Cundeelee became a mission station there was
a government official living there who doled out the few
government rations consisting of flour, sugar, tea, a tin of
meat and chewing tobacco in exchange for cutting and
cleaning a valuable commodity for the Asian market -
sandalwood.

According to the aborigines, he was not known for
his benevolent behavior. He not only had a mean dog, but

also carried a gun on his hip, which he had not been slow to use.

As time passed and the mantel of being the headman at Cundeelee began to settle on Bob, things subtly began to change – nothing drastic, just an air about the place. Bob and Ethel did not believe in telling the aborigines what they could or should not do, for they felt that was not their job. They were not there to "mold" them into replicas of themselves, change their culture, or way of life. They just wanted to share the good news of a God who loved them. It was all about the heart, or as this first group of Wangkatha people said – the stomach. Bob and Ethel were there to help, serve, tell of and show love to, these people others despised.

The aborigines did not in any way welcome the early missionaries who arrived at Cundeelee. Their faces were the same color as the ones who so often not only hunted them, but also used them for forced labor. In the beginning, all they saw was the same "whiteness of skin" and figured more cruel taskmasters had arrived.

The foreign-born missionaries, who were there in the early years, often struggled to understand the situation into which they had been "dropped." They were stunned when the aborigines cowed and trembled when in their presence.

It was not long though before the people took note that the missionaries had neither guard dogs nor weapons on their persons – no guns or stockmen's whips. Their first glimpse of a rifle in Bob's hands had sent them all running in terror. They were disconcerted and suspicious when he returned in the jeep with several freshly killed kangaroo, which he shared with everyone. They were bewildered when he worked along side them when cleaning and hauling sandalwood.

The hurt they had over loved ones who had been mistreated and/or killed by people of Bob's coloring made them wary. They accepted what he gave, but stayed fearful of what he might do to them.

It took years of watching, working alongside, snitching tools, spitting in his face, having a corroboree at the same time he was trying to hold a camp meeting and multiple other ploys before they would truly understand he served a God of Love.

Eventually, and long after the acceptance of Bob's children, and wife Pina Lyunku, Uncle Bob became "Tjamu" and accepted fully as "one of them."

It took more than two years before Bob would learn why the people avoided one area – one tree in particular – on the mesa where a few "white fella" houses had been built. By now, Bob had also received an aboriginal name, but his was more of a respectful title, for it was Tjamu or grandfather. Depending on the circumstances and person speaking to him, he was also referred to as Kurta (brother), however; most of the time he was greeted or addressed as "Uncle Bob."

One day an elder came close and motioned for "Tjamu" to follow him, then led him over to this tall dead tree, which had an unusually long thick branch running parallel to the ground. Others gathered – not too close - to watch the proceedings from a safe distance.

As Bob wondered what it was all about, he looked from the tree back to the elderly man who was now standing underneath it pointing with his lower lip, which signaled that Tjamu was to look up.

Bob moved nearer in order to discover what was being shared with him. Closer examination revealed several deep grooves. His first thoughts were that a swing had once been there, but that would not account for the fear he had witnessed on their faces whenever they neared this tree. Looking back down into the upturned face of this barely five foot elder, Bob noticed his lower lip point up at the tree and then down to his wrists which he held out in front of him and then down to his ankles.

On seeing Bob's furrowed brow, the old man's hands went into play and grabbing an ankle, he made as if to hoist it up to the tree limb and said, "Up there." Then Bob sensed someone beside him, felt the light brush of a finger on his arm, and heard a voice whisper, "Uncle Bob, if someone did anything to displease the white man, he used to chain the wrists or the ankles and leave the person dangling from this tree in the hot sun all day."

As they watched, his face first expressed unbelief, next understanding, followed by sorrow. They now gathered around to show him the various scars on their bodies. Now he knew why they had watched him so carefully and at times fearfully; he knew he had to do something.

After mulling things over a few days, talking and praying with Ethel concerning the situation, Bob sought out the old men. He asked them to set up a meeting, and that the most fluent English speaking man be present as well.

He wanted to make sure he was understood by all, and that no misunderstanding take place, for he knew his response to their hurts and sorrow was crucial.

The meeting in camp was set for a time when the day's hunting was over and every man would be present.

Bob lowered his 6' frame down onto the soft red dusty soil under the shade of a gum tree near Toby, Sinclair, Long Jack, Frank, and Jock. He then noticed the young men Don and Colin and knew he had his interpreters. (He often called them his interrupters.)

After the customary time of silence, allowing the area to become accustomed to their presence, a small cough signaled that it was now okay for their "Kurta" (and/or) Tjamu to speak his mind.

"Ngayulu ngaru," he said, beginning in their dialect. He wanted them to know he was so very sorry for what they had endured at the hands of another person with a white face like his. Having carefully watched his face when they'd shared their stories, they knew he was speaking from his heart and motioned that they understood what he said was true and to continue.

Taking a deep breath and saying a silent prayer for wisdom, he wondered yet again - how best could he explain the event he had in mind? It was not that he considered their intellect at fault, but their lack of celebrating in the way most of the rest of the world celebrates.

45

Such important days as Anzac Day, Christmas, Easter, Fourth of July, New Years, or Birthday celebration to the taking of a vacation – they knew none of these. They had never had the luxury of just the joy of taking a holiday; each day was serious business and one must find enough to eat, or go to bed hungry. They did have rituals and ceremonies at certain times when they all got together, but the essence or deeper meaning he wanted to convey was what needed explaining.

He started in again and this time Don and Colin helped and hindered each other trying to translate the heart or meaning of the suggestion or plan.

Tjamu wanted a memorial ceremony and a bonfire – at which time they would completely and totally burn down that tree. It would be "a sing" (really chanting) complete with damper smothered in golden syrup, which would be washed down with strong billy tea, sweetened with lots of sugar, and flavored by adding Sunshine powdered milk.

Other men gathered and sat with the decision making group while the women were seated further away almost out of sight. Everyone was interested in learning what "Tjamu" had to say. Soft guttural sounds of communication broke out, vying with the birds, and a gentle breeze, which created a rustling noise in the eucalyptus leaves over Bob's head.

After a time he was told they would think and talk about what he had said and would let him know. It was not a decision to be made in haste. There were many things to be considered. The Elders all had to be in agreement that it was a good idea to follow Uncle Bob's plan, for one did not lightly "mess" with the evil spirits' domain.

If lightning had struck the tree and burned it down - that would have been acceptable for nature would have taken over. It would have been out of their control and therefore they would not (in their mind) suffer any consequence due to its demise. There were many taboos that Tjamu did not know about or understand that would need to be dealt with. Even to the decision of who would be willing to deliberately go against custom and start the fire to burn down this hated tree.

It was one thing, or natural, to be afraid of an evil thing, but these were serious and weighty discussions about a deliberate act to get rid of it. If Uncle Bob had said to chop it down and then burn it, no one would have agreed. But fire? Maybe.

The nulla-nullas (tapping sticks) started the proceedings and several of the men who not many years before had spent days hanging upside down from the tree, were chosen to start the fire.

This act took much courage and faith in Uncle Bob's God. To them this was an evil tree, and one did not mess with the evil spirits unless you wished to invite sickness or trouble upon you and your tribe.

The tapping sticks temporarily went silent as their friend Uncle Bob stepped forward. He prayed to Mamakuurti in Heaven and His Son Jesus to heal their sorrows and protect them now and in time to come from all harm regarding this tree.

Once again, the sticks started to talk the chanting began. The fire was lit and what a beautiful sight it was to behold – just perfect for roasting marshmallows, and wieners, but this case to boil the billy, and later cook damper in the hot coals.

It was due to Bob's respect for the original people of the land that caused them to do something for him that they did not do for all missionaries. The old men came to Bob on the quiet, asking that he come to camp for a special ceremony. He was not to bring anyone else, nor tell the others what he would see.

They conveyed that they had watched him closely since he had arrived three years earlier, and were now convinced that he was different from others. Uncle Bob treated them like equals. He taught and trusted them to drive the truck, allowed his children to play with their children, fed them from the same plates he and his family ate from, and invited them to eat at his table.

When any of them were sick, Uncle Bob made every attempt to get them a ride in the passenger carriage of the train – instead of in the open on a flat car. When he was handing out rations, he had no gun. He did not own a dog whose purpose was to terrorize them.

He listened to their concerns and took them seriously. In fact, he treated each old woman as if she were his own mother, the young women like his sisters and the children as if they were his own. When his wife had a baby, he brought her to live among them and allowed the women to carry his son around and to feed him damper that they had made themselves. Yes, they had decided he was one of them – it was time for them to make that official.

After the ceremony, he would be related to each member of the tribe, as would his wife and each of his children. They would explain it all later, but it was enough for him to know now that his would not include all of their normal initiation practices.

His would be a unique honor/welcome to the tribe ceremony. They understood how much Uncle Bob loved Mamakuurti and because they wanted to honor "Tjamu" – they would be careful not do anything in this ceremony which would offend either.

Amid considerable secrecy and with a great deal of prayer, Bob went with the men. As far as we know, he never divulged the details of the events of those hours, but when he returned it was with a sense of having been highly honored.

Bob told his family in confidence, that they too had been admitted into the tribe, and tried to convey what that meant for them. Marilyn and Stephen, being the two youngest, had always mingled freely with everyone in camp and lived by their rules. They both felt loved and accepted and had never realized, until then, the advantage they'd had over their Dad, Mum, Darlene and Dale.

Author's notes:

In 2002, the author again spent some time in the outback of Western Australia talking with many tribal friends. Each one voiced singly and as a group, how Cundeelee is a very special place. It is not their primary homeland, as is Koolgahbin or Illdune or even similar in the feeling they have for Uluru (Ayers Rock), but it is a place where they would all like to live. To their minds, the area has retained the essence of Mamakuurti's presence.

To the aboriginal, Ayers Rock or Uluru is a very special place, but evokes a completely different meaning, essence, and feel, because it is a sacred place of their heritage and legends.

To my knowledge, Cundeelee is the only area these Spinifex aborigines deem as being so very special. For many it was the first time they were treated as human beings - on the same plane as a person with a white face. They basked in the welcome and acceptance they were given, but it was and is much deeper than airy-fairy feelings that are here today and gone tomorrow.

Cundeelee is a truly holy (as in good) place in that they really feel the presence of Mamakuurti living there. As you will read in the following stories – it was there that for the first time they witnessed good triumphing over evil.

It is the place where most of them for the first time heard about the God who loves them and experienced daily that love in action through the lives of many dedicated missionaries.

My friends/my tribe of Spinifex aboriginals are especially in tune with the forces around them, and I am encouraged that the Fragrance of Christ lingers long as He continues to draw them to Himself.

Church Service

Hunting Party

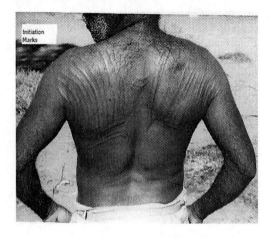

Initiation Marks

Cursing & Consequences

Words float around me, and I find
What I believe will rule my mind.

Many people think uncivilized people or primitive tribes are the only ones who truly believe in superstitions, the pronouncing of curses, or perform strange rituals.

Bob and Ethel came from middle class America, yet they were acquainted with many superstitions – even if they were not referred to as such.

Breaking a mirror is equal to seven years' bad luck

Step on a crack you'll break your mother's back

To continue having good luck throw salt over your left shoulder

Never walk under a ladder

Never open an umbrella in the house

Peel an apple continuously, then throw the peel over your shoulder and it would give you the initial of the person you were going to marry

Never leave a rocking chair – rocking

Beware a black cat crossing your path, and after three – turn around and go home

Beware the number 13 – as in Friday or a room or floor of a hotel.

To some people these were just words or phrases; however, to others they were a way of life. These and other mandates were strongly adhered to in Bob's family. It was because these "innocent sayings" so ruled the lives of some of their relatives that Bob and Ethel would be able, in a small way, to understand the hold words could have over a person.

Bob was not aware of the grip "warding off bad luck" had over him. He had grown up with these actions being drilled into him and now they were automatic. It was due in part to this history of avoiding bringing wrath or trouble upon himself or his family that he would be so affected by the angry words of his mother. He failed to understand her concerns and the frustration she felt at being unable to influence his decision to leave.

His mother was distraught over losing her son and grandchildren to a God-forsaken place. In a last ditch effort to deter them from going she pronounced many catastrophic ways in which they would all die. Those words of his mother would haunt not only him, but also his children and grandchildren for years to come.

It was because of the struggle he faced in dealing with the long-term effect of her words that Bob would have empathy with the aborigines and their fears regarding curses. He knew the reality that spiritual darkness has a mind-griping power; however, and more importantly he had experienced, over and over again – peace of mind and release from fear. As he searched the scriptures he would read how Jesus healed people - and the scripture that states (1 John 4:4b), – "greater is He (the Holy Spirit) that is in you than he (Satan) that is in the world."

For the primitive aboriginal, fear was an integral part of every day life - not only of the power of evil spirits, but also of the witch doctor. Pronouncing curses on people was one of his devious talents. His power and ability were undeniable. People lived in mind-warping fear of seeing an imprint referred to as "feather foot" near their sleeping area.

Bob and Ethel went to sleep only after prayer and committing their family into God's care because chanting and shouts meant another corroboree was taking place. Many nights it started simply as chanting and dancing only to escalate into fights and strange rituals. In the morning, the marks of "feather foot" having been around were evident. Sometimes after one of these "visits", a person disappeared never to be seen again.

One day, when Bob and Ethel had been there a long time and finally gained their trust, a man came running up to tell them that a certain individual was going to die. Having seen the fit and healthy young man the day before Bob queried - was it due to a spear and could he help in any way? After glancing around furtively, checking the area, the bearer of the news leaned toward Bob and whispered, "The witch doctor pointed the bone at him - he will die in two days."

The "victim" did not wish for Uncle Bob to pray for him for he knew he would die. The witch doctor/feather foot had cursed him with death. He had witnessed others die because of cursing, and knew his time was up. Fear - unreasoning and terrifying gripped his mind to the extent that in two days, he was dead.

As time passed, the aborigines witnessed how Mamakuurti protected the missionaries and how they prayed about everything - a shift in power began to be seen.

One day after Bob had been welcomed into the tribe some of the elders came asking that he go with them. Little by little, they began to share with him their ways and secrets. They became bold, in that now they considered him part of the tribe, and invited him to one of the men only events. It would be an unforgettable day – for all.

Each time Bob left for a "get together" Ethel prayed.

Usually the witch doctor preferred that Bob stay away from where he was operating. Over time having heard many stories of God's power, he grew bold. Wanting to impress Bob he invited him to a display of his power. Bob stayed on the edge of the gathering and began to pray for he felt a foreboding in his spirit of what was to come.

Each time the witch doctors' magic just started to work – such as a person floating – it would stop. No matter how hard the witch doctor tried, he could not complete the action. Things the others had never seen fail were now brought to an abrupt halt. He finally cried out, "Uncle Bob, leave us! Your God's power is too strong. He stops the spirits from working. Leave us!"

Bob was glad to leave the area for the things he had witnessed scared him. However, once again he and all the men there had witnessed the truth of the verse, "Greater is He that is in you than he that is in the world." This day signaled a turning point, for they had been eyewitnesses to Mamakuurti's strength. They were beginning to understand Bob served the God who loved them.

Author's notes:
In the fall of 1956 upon returning from Australia, we lived in Seattle for a couple of months. We were fascinated with grandmother's rocking chair and loved to set it in motion. We had no idea of the fear it stirred up, but quickly learned never to leave a rocking chair rocking.

At Cundeelee, it would cloud up, the thunder and lightening would scare me half to death, the rain soaked me to the skin and it would be over for months. However, in Seattle it would rain for a week at a time. I watched how people opened their umbrellas, but had not thought the "where" to be problem until I experimentally opened one in the house. How could I know this innocent activity would cause such a fear of disaster falling upon their home? I was crushed to know I had done something wrong, but accepted the rebuke as meaning I had offended the spirits. I now knew that here one had to be as careful as in my beloved outback.

Whether we like it or not words from others greatly affect us emotionally. I have seen both long-term adverse effects from harsh words and incredible accomplishments from others who were given encouragement.

This story was shared to heighten your awareness of the power of the spoken word. Words can encourage or intimidate - bless or curse – cause laughter or tears. They even have the power to hold you captive. God is interested in the words you think, say, and choose to believe.

"May the words of my mouth and the meditation of my heart be pleasing in your sight, O Lord, my Rock and my Redeemer." Psalm 19:14 (NIV)

Buried & Believing

Buried yet I was still alive,
Fear was rampant, would I survive?

Taking a morning tea break from cutting and cleaning sandalwood with my companions, one suddenly blurts out, "Uncle Bob, remember when we buried you?"

My lips curve into a smile as I softly say "Uwa" (yes) and shiver as I recall the nights since then I've bolted up from sleep to find I am confined only by a twisted sheet. In an instant I am back in time. How many times since then I had relived these hours.

I remember thinking throughout that day - today I had made the worst decision in my entire life!

No clouds, trees, or even scrub brush to be seen, and it feels as if the temperature rises yet another degree with each step I take. The day so far has seemed endless for we have been walking since before sun up and it is now nearing noon.

In trying to protect myself as much as possible from the intense rays of the suns I am almost totally hidden by apparel. The lightweight Pith helmet not only protects my head, but also shades my ears and eyes. The turned up collar on my coveralls protects my neck, and I alternate between tucking my hands down into the pockets and withdrawing them back up into the long sleeves.

At first as I walked, I swung my hands by my sides and as a result, they are badly sun burned. My feet are encased as usual in heavy work boots made especially for me by my father. It feels as if sores are forming on top of open blisters on my toes and heels.

My stomach is in a knot due to both fear and hunger, my mouth is parched due to lack of water, and yet I continue plodding, albeit ever slower, in the wake of three other men. I am way past the point of being tired and weary. I am even past the point of total exhaustion, and it is only my will to live that is keeping me traveling slowly forward. I know that unless a miracle takes place in the next several hours this will be my last day alive on this earth.

I am so well covered that it would be hard to guess at my skin color and that is part of my problem for I am fair skinned or "white" and not used to such searing dry heat. I squint peering ahead, through burning and blurring eyes, at my three dark skinned companions. I am again amazed at their resilience. All morning they have not even seemed to notice the extreme heat, and the scorching sand has not blistered their bare feet.

At first we walked over rocks heated by the sun, and now for what seems like hours, we've trudged through scorching sand dunes of soft red soil. My aboriginal companions are way ahead of me and still show no signs of slowing, or of any bodily distress. On the other hand, every part of my body is just short of being in extreme agony. For the last hour, a seed of fear has blossomed inside my mind choking out a lot of my physical misery at being so hot and thirsty. We are surrounded by silty, fine red soil with not a rock to be found.

A while back in desperation, I thought to break the threads holding one of the buttons on my coveralls and placed it in my mouth to suck on in the hopes of getting a little saliva to form.

We desperately need to find water and very soon. This last hour I have come to realize how much I am slowing them down and feel as though another mile even will be beyond my physical ability. I can barely think due to the pounding, throbbing, aching in my head. I have heard of migraines, and my wife suffers acutely when she gets a headache, but I rarely get so much as a twinge; this is brutal!

Raising my chin just a little and squinting through smarting eyes, I look ahead, blink and focus on a couple of trees and a few shrubs less than a quarter of a mile away.

"Oh, joy! Some shade," and *"Thank you Lord,"* are my thoughts, which remain unspoken for my tongue is too swollen and my mouth too dry to rasp out a single word.

As I struggle to keep my balance and put one foot in front of the other for the last hundred feet to the shade, I dimly realize there is a heated, though not loud, discussion going on between my three companions.

At the first bit of shade, I drop to the ground and fold into a heap of complete and utter exhaustion. Never in my life had I, Robert Stanley Stewart, felt so beaten by the elements and let down by my strong body. I am shocked at how quickly my body has weakened without the nourishment of water. After lying still for several minutes, I feel the slightest of breezes touch my face and perspiration-drenched coveralls. It revives my spirits just a little.

I think of my companions and move my head a fraction in order to check on where and what my aboriginal friends are doing. With eyelids barely parted, I try to focus my painfully burning eyes in the direction of the noise they are making.

The men, having laid aside their spears and boomerangs, are in the shade between a small shrub and a tree digging fast and furiously in the soft sand. Wondering what is going on I force my sore eyes to continue watching.

Oh, my, I really do not like the look of what is taking place. They are no longer continuing to dig downward as if for water. I am overwhelmed with a terrible foreboding. I wonder if it is just my fevered imagination that the length and breath of this hole appears to be just my size for I am larger in every way than my three friends. The hole has suddenly taken on the appearance of a grave. I wonder if I have I offended them in some way.

I thought of these aborigines as my friends even though as yet I didn't understand much of their culture, language, or way of life nor they mine. They seem to be motioning for me to come over to them. I desperately wish I could understand what they are saying to each other. I try to *push myself up off the ground, rise and walk the few feet to them.*

I am normally a healthy, athletic, strong young man in my prime; but try, as I will, I cannot stand up. Next, I try to crawl towards them. Again, the effort is beyond my capability. It is humbling to be as weak as a baby. I am almost, but not quite, beyond caring what happens to me in the next couple of minutes or hours. I am past being able to do anything to save myself from whatever their plans are regarding me. Wearily I sag the few inches to the ground.

Seeing I cannot do what they ask, all three come over, gently lift me up, and carefully lay me down into the hole. I struggle briefly, then lay still as they straighten out my legs and quickly start covering me with the loose soil. As they work, they talk very softly in their guttural sounding language. Whether it is to each other or to me, I am not sure for they do not look at me.

In minutes, their task is complete. I lay at a slant with the back of my head resting relatively comfortably on a specially created earthen pillow. Only the front of my neck and my head protrude from this grave of well-packed dirt.

I reason to myself, "They mean for me to die very slowly." I am not sure if I am relieved that they did not bury me totally or kill me outright. At the same time, I wonder if I am man enough to endure whatever lies ahead.

I peer up hopelessly at them, and see them give me a sign for what I think means, "to sit down," and wryly think "that's a laugh for I'm obviously not going anywhere."

Now they are hurrying – one retrieves my hat, which had fallen off when they had moved me, another sweeps the area using a branch, while the third one takes time to drop leaves and twigs here and there. I watch as six eyes check the area around me and beyond. In a final act, my hat is placed on my head and given a light downward push to ensure it is snugly in place.

I have just been buried alive. The silence suddenly becomes almost unbearable for I know they have left and I am totally alone. I am in the huge outback of Western

Australia where one can go for hundreds of miles in any direction and never see another person. Only three people in the world know my situation and exact location, and they are from another culture, language, and race.

Waves of fear grip my mind until I'm suddenly reminded that while it is true only three people in the whole world know my mind-warping predicament, it is also true that The Most High God, creator of the universe knows.

After a time new thoughts and fears race through my anxious mind trying to completely overwhelm my sanity. I am on the verge of total panic when the words "The Lord Is My Shepherd" come to mind. Fragments of other verses float through my head reminding me of God's love and care. They calm my thoughts, comfort my heart, and bring peace to my mind.

My mind wanders back in time to that life changing prayer. It set in motion the chain of events that brought me to where I am today. Here I am alone, buried deep enough so I can't even swat at a fly, dying of thirst, totally at the mercy of an unmerciful desert, and thinking none of my family will ever know what happened to me.

In spite of the heat, I feel a chill run down my spine as I think of the variety of ways I could die out here, for this is a wild land full of the deadliest of snakes and spiders in the world. My list grows as I think of the ants, centipedes, goannas, scorpions, and wild dingo, any of which could make my end even more painful than just dying of dehydration and thirst.

With the passing of each hour, I am learning that fear and praying cannot both occupy my mind at the same time. I battle with staying conscious for I do not wish to relinquish my last bit of control. Silently I pray, "Before I drift off again Lord, this is a huge world in which only you and three humans know where I am, and I'm not one of them. I desperately need your intervention."

The hours are passing so slowly. My mind drifts back in time once again to the night only a few years ago when I promised God that if he'd see fit to make a miracle happen *and save both my wife and baby, I'd search for Him and serve Him for the rest of my life. I, in turn, had fulfilled my promise to search for Him. In time, I had come to believe that the Bible was God's Holy Scripture. Words cannot explain the peace and joy that had overwhelmed me then. Strangely enough, the same peace is coursing through me in the midst of this incredible situation.*

Memories, faces of family and friends revolve hazily on the screen of my mind. I am finding it increasingly hard to concentrate. I drift in and out of consciousness.

This morning – was it only this morning that this struggle to continue living had started in earnest? Ah, yes, I hazily remember, and then I am suddenly and rudely jarred awake with a terrible thought. I must bear the responsibility, for I had insisted on coming along. We had broken down and run out of water in the middle of nowhere and they had wished to leave me by the jeep, while they went to find water. They knew where to locate the trees with water in their roots.

If my eyes and body were not devoid of water, tears would have streamed down my face at the thought that my friends might not make it to water. My imminent death was no longer important as I grieved lest my –oh-so-very-good intentions would end in their deaths.

I had always prided myself in not asking anyone to do anything that I was not willing to do or had not done myself. At the time, I had been sincere in my belief it was the right thing to do, but now saw clearly it masked the sin of pride. I began praying for forgiveness and no longer for my rescue, but for my aboriginal friends.

I did promise God that if I lived I would tell my friends how truly sorry I was for not taking the advice they'd drawn and mimed for my understanding that very morning. I determined in future, if I survived, to listen to others' points of view and weigh their ideas much more carefully.

It feels as if I've been entombed for days – yet it has only been hours since my companions left me here incapacitated. The shadows are lengthening, it is definitely not as hot as it was, and I am guessing in an hour, two at the most, it will be very dark, and my vulnerability will increase. I know these aboriginal people, at least the ones we live with, rarely-to-never venture out after dark, and many desert creatures sleep in the heat of the day and hunt at night.

My eyes and tongue are so dry and swollen I know I will never make it through the night unless a miracle takes place.

I am scared to just give up and allow myself to drift off, yet at the same time I am edgy and jumpy trying to maintain some sort of control. The only thing I have, to some degree, control over is my mind - so will continue endeavoring to stay alert.

I am praying for everyone I can think of in an effort to focus on anything and everything rather than the fear and pain of the present.

We had told God, "whatever, wherever," but it had been a scary, heart wrenching, and challenging plan to pack up and leave family and friends as well as a secure country (as far as living) for an unknown future in a completely foreign land.

There is still a deep hurt in my soul regarding the words my own mother hurled at us in hopes we'd change our minds and stay. Even now as I lay here, I am reminded of the various ways she had said we would die and now, except for God's intervention, she will have been proven right.

Even though my father had taught me how to make shoes, he had never wanted me to follow in his footsteps as it was hard work and little pay except for the satisfaction of having helped others. Maybe he understood a little, but he never said much about our going – just gave me a shoe last saying if I ever needed to make shoes, here was the means with which to do it.

The questions we heard so often, "Why do you have to go, and why so far away?" now return to torture my mind. Suddenly a new fear arises - what ever will happen to Ethel and the children?

I'd told God and meant it when I said I would serve Him. But never in my wildest imagination had I thought we *would be so far from our homeland or amongst such a primitive people.*

I think of how far we live from civilization, with no natural water source, of the constant demands and the daily, weekly and monthly struggle it takes just to survive. When I think of the aborigines, I realize that despite all of the problems, I'd rather be here sharing my life and the good news of a God who loves them than to be anywhere else.

Uncomfortable I involuntarily attempt to wriggle only to be instantly reminded that I'm still tightly confined under a mound of dirt. The increasing shadows tell of the sun nearing the horizon and the silence amplifies the lack of human voices.

My heart in desperation cries out "Oh, God, have You forsaken me? Do not forget You made me. You placed the desire in my heart to come and tell these people about You. How can I share Your good news with them if I die out here today? You were with us in Canada when there should have been snow, yet we came through on a dry road. You were with us when our plane was in imminent danger of crashing leaving Fiji yet miraculously lifted at the last possible moment."

"You have been with us in the start of a new work in the outback 156 miles from the nearest civilization, but close to the route used by these nomadic desert peoples. You have been with us in the healthy birth of our fourth child, here in Western Australia. Time and again you've provided rain or the money needed to buy water. Once again I ask for protection for my wife and children."

"Lord, I can't think straight. My eyes are swollen shut. My tongue is like a rock – hard and dry as a desert bone. I am in agony and not able to hang on any longer. May Your name be glorified, oh Lord."

Am I dreaming? Or hallucinating? Neither with my brain or my eyes can I bring anything into focus. Strangely familiar sounds vibrate in the still air near me. Had I really felt water trickling over my swollen and cracked lips?

I cannot stay awake long enough to assess my situation and drift off again. I become vaguely aware of a cool damp cloth covering my eyes. Oh, how weary I am!

All at once, I am fully conscious. As if through a haze, I see a faint orange glow. Is it sunset? Fear surges. Now I am worse off than before. I am alone and encased in my dirt coffin while spiders, scorpions, snakes and dingoes are beginning their prowl in search of prey.

I sense movement - something is near me. I take a shallow breath then freeze. The cloth is being removed. I feel a light touch near my mouth and water trickling down my throat. It had not been a dream!

Out of the darkness, I hear "Uncle Bob, Uncle Bob?" It was a familiar voice. They had returned!

My headache had eased, and although my throat still felt as dry as dust, my tongue was definitely not as swollen. I could move it – just barely. After resting a bit I try checking my surroundings again. I turn my head slightly and peek through barely opened eyelids. Out of the corner of my eye I can see light from a small fire. Huddled near it I see silhouettes of three individuals. My eyes soon become accustomed to the darkness only to find it was not as dark as I had at first thought.

The moon is high in the sky and the brilliance and multitude of stars is breathtakingly magnificent. I cannot remember the last time I stopped long enough to drink in their incredible beauty.

Once again, I try to speak, only to hear my voice as a raspy whisper. After looking at me and glancing at each other, without a word being spoken, they kneel down and scoop away the confining earth.

Even when most of the dirt has been removed, it is impossible for me to move my limbs. My companions lift me up and out of the hole and gently lower me to the ground half way between the now open trench and the fire. Although my first response is relief, it is quickly followed by a twinge of concern. There have been stories of cannibalism amongst this tribe. It flashes through my mind that maybe they would move the fire into the hole and cook me. (I had seen them cook emus and kangaroo in just such holes.) My mind is alternating between fear and relief as they start massaging my limbs. Numbness becomes pins and needles and unbelievable pain as circulation returns. Finally, I am finally able to move my legs.

Gradually I am convinced they mean me no harm. It is during this time that their loving care finally penetrates my soul and grips my mind. All fear of these primitive stone-age aboriginal people is gone.

They are more than friends.

Truly, they are my brothers.

"Uncle Bob," "Uncle Bob," brought me back with a start to the present, and I realized they wanted to talk and share their side of the story with me.

"Uncle Bob, you were slowing us down and we were afraid. We were afraid to leave you and afraid not to – that is what we were arguing about. There was no way you could keep up with us, and if we slowed down any more, then we would all have died. We could have traveled faster, but had hung back so you could see us all morning.

We were fussing over what to do with this "white man" – for his own good. We were afraid to "lay hands" on you and put you in that hole – to help you, because of your white skin. Uncle Bob, you know what many "white skins" do to our people – for no reason at all."

I nod silently and sorrowfully for I have seen and heard much regarding their ill treatment and deaths.

"We also didn't want to upset the spirits that you came here to tell us about – you know – the good ones who love us. We knew you were a good man sent to us by Mamakuurti (God) who lives in Heaven, so for a while we did not know what we should do. Your eyes got so big (graphically demonstrated) when you saw us digging that hole. We knew you thought bad thoughts of what we were going to do to you, but there were three reasons we did it.

You now understand we did it to save your life, but we want you to understand everything.

"We buried you in your wet clothes to keep you moist and from getting any more dehydrated.

"We had to bury you because your scent was really bad and because of that you would attract wild animals, but the ground would save you by eating up the smell.

"The last reason we buried you was for your sake as well as ours. In your delirium, we were afraid you might wander off and knowing we would be coming back at or after dark it would take us longer to find you, but by burying you we knew exactly where to look.

"Uncle Bob, you sure had us scared, for when we got back we thought you were dead for sure. We poured a little water in your mouth just in case and your tongue twitched ever so slightly. We knew then that the Good God, you talk about, and who lives in heaven was looking after you and that you would live.

"We know you didn't figure it out that day, but we said, 'Wait here and when we find water we will come back for you!'"

(Slapping a hand against his leg) "Uncle Bob, your eyes sure got big a lot that day."

Everyone laughs - Ha! Ha! Ha!

By now, what tea is left in our mugs is cold. Out of the comfortable reflective silence first one then another whisper a request and a question.

"Tell us once again about Mamakuurti and His Son Jesus who lives high above the stars and in hearts.
They know all about us?
They love us?
Truly?"

Life & Living

Life is from God the true author of giving,
Love and obedience beget a fragrance so winning.

Bob and Ethel had many exciting adventures, but as with everyone most of their days were filled with many routine jobs, as well as situations to be resolved.

Working and interacting with a primitive tribe they found was very different from living with a civilized one. In the early years at Cundeelee, there was mainly the Wangkatha tribe of which only some had a little knowledge regarding white man's ways. Other than moral ethics, which were amazingly close to the Ten Commandments recorded in the Bible, their culture itself was very different.

Life was so simple; our life very plain,
It was in relationships where we really gained.
Our lifestyle was communal; from birth we did train
Our eyes and our minds to look past our pain
Each moment each day we lived under the strain
To provide for our clan in this desert - dry terrain.

We didn't settle permanently on any piece of land,
But we did wander at will across hot desert sand.
We didn't grow crops; our diet mostly bland,
But we did hunt and gather, according to each clan.
We didn't know about minerals, or for gold to pan,
But we did track for hours, be it animal or man.

We didn't carry matches or blazing fire sticks,
But we did make fire, a kangaroo meal to fix.
We didn't build houses or even make a brick,
But we did make weapons that deliver quite a kick.
We didn't see mosquitoes, or even know a tick,
But we have enough flies to make us really sick!

Much of our talk was done just by mime.
We never saw money, not even one thin dime.
No fruits had we tasted, neither apple nor lime,
A person turned twenty, was now in his prime.
Bloodshed was the law, for an offense or a crime;
Only today (the now), did we understand as time.

We feared the night, lived with no hint of song;
Our tapping sticks sounded hollow, just like a gong.
We looked into the heavens, at the starry throng.
We wanted to know the good God; for this we did long.
We knew the evil devil, and that we'd done wrong,
But oh, how to the good God, we wish we belong.

Bob and Ethel came to tell us, of the good God's awesome plan,
And how it makes no difference, whether I'm a woman or a man.
This news brings such comfort, for its message is so grand;
We can have a glad assurance, when in eternity we stand,
Before the Holy God and the angelic heavenly band.
Good works and money cannot buy this, but simple faith can.
Marilyn Stewart

For thousands of years they had traveled pretty much only in their separate little world, and in small groups or clans. Discipline, rank, and file had been easy to maintain as certain things were taboo, just as certain walkabout areas were used by different tribes.

Things began changing at Cundeelee with the testing at the Woomera Rocket Range in the 1950's and Ooldea Mission in South Australia closing. The mix became even more fluid as more stone-age primitive Spinifex aborigines made their way to Cundeelee. The arrival of each tribe/clan and dialect made mediation even more of a challenge, for things could and often did get dicey very quickly.

While they roamed and hunted in their designated areas inland, they did not suffer from malnutrition, but stayed slim and fit. They were encouraged to continue this way of life while at Cundeelee, but some things had to be relearned. For instance, 250 miles inland the Witchetty grub at a certain season of the year is to be found under the bark of a Ghost Gum tree, whereas in the area around Cundeelee the grub worm was found in the roots of a certain shrub.

The rule at Cundeelee was that one had to work for extra food or such things as matches and tools. There are always a few in every culture who try to cut corners, and here it was no different. For instance, if an elder told a child he "liked" his/her tin of food, then the child was required to hand it over. Fights tended to break out over anything and everything, but especially over meat and women.

There were certain times that "the law"/men's ceremonies were held elsewhere. The men had many rituals, which the women were forbidden to witness, and if they did deliberately peek, their tracks would betray them and they'd be severely punished or more likely speared to death. They had an intricate set of rules and laws, which governed every aspect of their lives. Just as a city has housing codes and standards so did they. The location, and situation of each shelter was predetermined by law and weather conditions.

People came and went from Cundeelee, depending on the time of year, and what was going on. Others just had that restless feeling that prompted them to go walkabout. Then the numbers of aborigines at Cundeelee would drop significantly – sometimes from 100 people to 10.

Primitive aborigines are accustomed to being fully aware of their surroundings. Nothing transpired without their knowledge: Seeing, hearing, smelling, feeling, and sensing everything around them is an essential part of their way of life. Being in a walled house filled them with dread.

Every couple of days Aboriginal men hunted for large game such as kangaroo and emu. A big feed of meat would tide them over for several days. The women on the other hand spent part of every day gathering berries, eggs, roots, seeds, grubs, and lizards. Even so they were considered to be of less value than a hunting dog and grew up with this mindset. The aboriginal babies, almost all of the time, were carried by their mothers.

From sun up to just before dusk each day, Ethel was kept very busy. In addition to her household duties and caring for her new baby, Ethel supervised the correspondence lessons of her three older children. People came asking for band-aids and cough medicine. Ethel spent hours treating infected sores, cuts, the occasional burn, assisting mothers with their babies, and washing eyes glued shut with conjunctivitis. One man came every day for years to soak his ulcerated heel and have it bandaged. Her lack of medical knowledge coupled with the inability to contact a doctor, was a frightening responsibility, and extremely stressful.

One frustration for Ethel was the lack of water: Water to drink, to bathe, to cook, not to mention to wash clothes – especially the baby's nappies. Whether the call was in regards to pneumonia or a breach baby she endeavored to do her very best. Ethel endured despite often feeling over-whelmed. She struggled with her own health related issues including frequent headaches, not to mention the dry climate, hordes of flies, lack of proper housing. Sometimes, when Ethel was exhausted, daughter Darlene often stepped in to assist her.

Native Welfare officers liked to drop in unannounced hoping to find something amiss. They would stop in camp first, to see how the aborigines were faring, but someone usually ran up to rat them out. Next, they would check to see if Bob was up to date with the entries in their books.

If there were enough daylight, they would go out to see how the cutting and cleaning of the sandalwood was progressing or if it needed some prodding. All the while, they watched Bob and the way he treated the aborigines. One never knew what would transpire during their visit. It ranged from sharp words to stony silence; a worthwhile conversation shared, to a commendation; or an amazed comment regarding the work he had "gotten out of them" without the use of force.

Author's notes:

Dad and Mum were two normal human beings who often felt trapped due to economic and culturally created problems, their own inadequacies, and the feeling of being overwhelmed by the needs constantly surrounding them.

These were primitive people who had to learn about everything civilized people take for granted. For example, they did not know to take a top off of a child when they got soaked with rain and there was a bitterly cold wind. The very clothes Ethel had given them to keep the child warm, now she wanted to take back – or so they often thought. Auntie Ethel told them to put it on to keep the child warm. Then she told them to take it off or the child would get big-time sick. This new way of life had too many strange rules.

In time, the primus stove was replaced, and Ethel had the luxury of cooking on a huge stove. It even had a reservoir for water, but the down side was the heat it put out – especially during summer when there was no way to cool down the house.

In 2002 when I went inland to the Aboriginal Community at Tjuntjuntjara, I was delighted to see a new building that bore the label, "Women's Center." The women are being taught all kinds of things from arts and crafts to food preparation. I saw hand made cards, baskets, dot paintings; curtains finished using a method called batik, as well as several well-done sewing projects.

Some of the aboriginal men came to look through the new building and after seeing all of the things the women were learning to make said, "We need something also." The men have had a workshop in the past, but most need constant supervision for they are like loose, unschooled children. They have no idea of how to use the tools correctly and safely, nor do they comprehend the dangers and damage they can inflict on their bodies so very quickly.

Marilyn Stewart

It will take time, repeated demonstrations, much patience, and constant monitoring, but in time (and time is definitely the key) they will succeed.

SANDALWOOD

Food!

72

Water & Well

**Help lay asleep under a nearby tree,
While deep in the hole, one knelt, on bended knee.**

When one lives one hundred fifty six miles from the nearest wells, or taps that turn and water flows, one tends to do everything in their power not only to conserve this precious commodity, but also try to find more of it.

In the 1950's, geologists and even a diviner or two came outback to assist in locating potential fresh water sites. They checked the soft red dirt area, in the rocky spots, where it was sandy, and even near the salt creek (which is reported to be seven times saltier than the ocean) five miles from Cundeelee. Several spots were picked as extremely promising. None of the "experts" hung around for the hard work that lay ahead, or to see whether or not their predictions were correct.

Bob's mind continued to wrestle with the fact that they desperately needed a well so they could not only stop having to pay for water, but also stop hauling it through the ever-changing desert. The jaunt was twenty-six miles one-way over shrubs, and spinifex, through sandhills, a salt creek, hardpan (unless it had rained) and soft red dirt.

Each trip was an adventure, an unending challenge to men and their machines as they followed a track consisting of a once graded road, headed to the railway line to pick up food and water supplies. This 52-mile excursion was made twice a week. The fast goods train headed east on Mondays and brought fresh bread, meat, and our mailbag. The Tea-and-Sugar came through Zanthus on Thursday nights carrying the groceries we had ordered the previous week.

Digging wells had to be sandwiched between other essential services requiring Bob's oversight. The old army ambulance and the jeep, which were crucial for hauling in the necessary food and water, had to be maintained. Housing for missionaries was always a critical issue, not to mention the difficulty of trying to find beds for the visitors.

Cundeelee was an out station where aborigines were free to come and go any time they so desired. When they were in camp many of the young men could be found working alongside their Uncle Bob. Stanley, Colin and Don loved to learn new things. After time, Bob began to entrust them with many tasks – such as helping to give out rations, driving a truck, and even hunting kangaroo using a rifle. [The sight of the latter terrified a visiting government official. After tearing strips off Bob, he hurriedly left.]

They had finally decided on a digging site. Now they could begin - digging by hand using the only tools they had - a shovel, a pick and a crowbar. They marked out a rectangle three foot by five foot and began. The men worked with a will for several days. One would use the pick then another got down and shoveled out the loosened rock and sand. They shored up the sides as they went. When they could no longer jump in and out, they constructed a bucket and pulley system to take them down into the well and to send up the debris.

One day Stanley did not show up for work. Bob just figured he had "gone walkabout" as they so often did, until later that afternoon when he saw him sitting near a fire in camp. Then a few days later Colin did not show up to dig at the well. Bob and Don continued together. Several days later Don became the third "no show" at the dig site. Bob could not recruit any others to help and so built a ladder and worked it himself. It was too much for one person alone, and Bob could not figure out what the problem was with the three young men who loved to help him.

At morning break, as Bob sat on the ground in the shade of a tree sipping his freshly poured tea – a strong brew of "billy" tea - he started reviewing the "facts" as he knew them to be. Each of these young men had ended up digging in the "well" the evening before they had quit. Bob had been down many times and seen nothing he could think of that could in anyway cause this behavior. Why had they quit helping and said nothing? They still came around, helped at the sandalwood pile and loading the truck, but each one stayed far away from the hole in the ground.

One day Bob had become so frustrated over the slow progress that he resorted to using dynamite. He had used it before so knew just how long to make the fuse to allow him sufficient time to climb the ladder to safety. He had not counted on a couple rungs on the ladder breaking. When he dropped to the bottom of the hole, Bob knew he was in trouble. With no tools to clamp the wire, he had no choice except to climb again - and quickly.

Grabbing the rope the bucket was normally attached to, he pulled himself up, hand over hand, until he was past the broken part of the ladder, and then he put all of his energy into racing up the steps as fast as he could. As he threw himself clear of the hole onto the ground, he only had time to raise his arms over his head before being rained upon by a shower of rocks. He was so thankful that before he had gone down the last time, he had undone and left the bucket at the top, but had absentmindedly thrown the rope back down into the well.

With his heart still thumping from his race to escape the well and the fright he had endured, he checked himself over finding that although he was badly bruised nothing was broken. His first whispered words were, "Thank you, Lord, for your protection this day."

Thanks to the blast, the ladder had a lot more damage than just two broken steps. After repairing it and returning down into the "pit" once again in hopes of finding water, he was disheartened, for all he found was more dry rubble. The well ate his energy and his time from other projects.

The hole eventually was too deep and unsafe for one person to work alone, and the air was getting thin and toxic making it downright dangerous. For a while, Bob had to give up and quit digging entirely.

Thinking there had to be a better, less labor-intensive way to find or store water, his mind ventured yet once more to possibilities and other alternatives.

There were two much larger than average rockholes – one five miles and one twelve miles from Cundeelee - that captured and held water runoff each time it rained. Bob thought it would be a good idea to enlarge or dig these out so the next time it rained, there would be more water available and everyone would benefit. The missionaries agreed that this was an excellent plan.

Fortunately for Bob, he was aware that this was not his land and always tried to act accordingly. So during one tea break he casually mentioned this plan to some of the older aboriginal men.

Oh! My! What a ruckus! Men were on their feet, tea forgotten, wardi and spears visible as they impressed upon Bob how these were sacred places and NOT to be disturbed. Whew! Good thing he had mentioned it.

Each intense dust storm that marched for hours, high and wide across the desert, decreased even more the amount of water these two natural rockholes could hold.

One day the elders of the tribe came to Uncle Bob and told him they had watched how he cared for them and their land. Because of this, they would give their permission to clean out the rockholes. It was taboo for any of them to do anything other than use the water that was found in these catchment basins after a rain; therefore, there was one condition attached. They would allow the rockholes to be tampered with if Uncle Bob and Uncle Bob only did, or at least supervised, the work. This showed a huge growth step for them to break with tradition.

Bob was grateful they finally trusted him enough to not desecrate their rockholes, and were allowing him to do something that not that long before would have resulted in bloodshed – namely his. He knew he was being honored by this special consideration to enlarge the hole and remove the debris. It would definitely mean more clean water for everyone. He would remove animal carcasses, dead wood, and sand that had accumulated down through the years. So he willingly added one more thing to his "to do list".

Early on the missionaries agreed to get at least one large tank at Cundeelee in which to store water. Each trip for supplies from the "Tea & Sugar" train that stopped at Zanthus was used to refill the tank on the truck yet again with water from the rail tanker. As more aboriginal folk arrived, went walkabout, and returned to Cundeelee making it their main campground, the need for water increased.

Bob asked the government officials in charge of Native Affairs in Kalgoorlie to help with the situation. Eventually he received, via the "Tea & Sugar" train, stacks of corrugated iron and bags of cement. It was billed to him and the mission.

Bob's background in math came in handy yet again when calculating how strong to make the base, for he surely didn't want it to collapse under the weight of a full tank of water. His engineering skills as well as puzzle solving were put to the test as he figured how the curved pieces of corrugated iron could be turned into a useful leak proof tank. Bob and Bert worked numerous eighteen-hour days figuring, cutting, riveting, and welding, before the tank was finally completed.

Bob felt a little of the pressure lift, for the tank was ready, as was a nearby dam they had dug. Although no rain had fallen, at least the water could now be pumped out of the tank on the truck and into the large newly completed stationary tank. Now, when the truck went to pick up their food supplies at the railhead, some twenty-six miles away, the people at Cundeelee had water. They no longer had to hope and pray quite so hard that the truck returned quickly.

Now that the square tank could be safely emptied, it could be taken off the truck bed between supply runs. The big truck could take a turn, sparing the jeep and small trailer numerous runs, by hauling a full load of cleaned sandalwood to Zanthus. There was always an empty rail car left on the siding for the express purpose of being loaded with sandalwood from Cundeelee. Bob found it was one way in which the aborigines could learn how to use white man's implements, earn some money, tools, or trade their hours worked for extra food rations.

They were tough years and each letter written (no phones or e-mail) had the following message – "Please Pray; we need rain desperately!" It was often two to three months between a letter being written at Cundeelee and received in Canada or the United States, but the need was still the same.

Bob told son Dale that he was the official "rain record keeper." Dale recorded only one fourth inch of rain in an eighteen-month period. It was DRY, it was HOT (like Phoenix) and Bob and Ethel still had no electricity.

While the sky was a beautiful blue, the heat was inescapable. Animals became scarce to find near Cundeelee. People arrived hungry and thirsty. The Stewart family took Saturday night baths often consisting of an all over wipe down using 3 or 4 cups of water. Long hair was washed just once a month and there was no such thing as conditioner. Ethel was hard pressed to make sure all water was boiled for at least twenty minutes before it was drunk. She had stopped asking what had been fished or strained out prior to pouring the water into the tin and bringing it to a boil on her stove.

Flies were everywhere and extremely persistent in trying to get "their own water" by sucking it out of every, and any, moist location they found. When mealtime arrived, Ethel had learned to place the children in strategic places. One raised the netting or cover while the others waved their hands in an often-vain attempt to ward off the flies. Ethel hated to prepare meat and have the blowflies drop their young (maggots) as they flew over, making her scrape or wash (depending on how much water there was) them off while hoping it wouldn't happen again during that meal. Bob, Ethel, and family learned to eat using only one hand while keeping the other in a constant waving motion endeavoring to keep the flies from contaminating their food.

Bob's thoughts constantly returned to the well that needed to be worked, and the three men who had quit so suddenly. One day all three fellows Bob had been thinking about came together for their "cuppa" and sat nearby under the same shade tree. They alternated between chatting quietly in their dialect and being silent while waiting for the billy to boil yet once more.

Now Bob, coming from Seattle, Washington with his Western point of view and approach to problem-solving wanted to ask them point blank, "Why did you stop working down in the well?"

The men who had been working with him came from thousands of years of nomadic wandering in the Inland of Western Australia's outback and their culture said, "Observe and learn," and did not question the *why* of anything.

Bob thought of how they were not familiar with work as he knew it. To them work had always been just two things. The first was finding food enough to survive and the second, making their own weapons. These, not so long ago primitive aborigines had to learn about, as well as how to use, every single thing he took for granted. It was like teaching children, for he had to repeat everything over and over again in the hope that over time copying would turn into comprehension. It was the same for him in regards to their culture, for as an adult he found it often very slow going in regards to his understanding of their culture and ways.

Having had many weeks in which to mull things over, Bob, now that the opportunity had arisen, casually asked the three if they would help him if they did not have to go down into the hole. After glancing at each other, they nodded in agreement. Silently they wondered if this was a trick. What did Uncle Bob want them to do if they did not go down into that cavity deep in the ground?

This was no prestigious college, but here Bob was always facing new challenges and endeavoring to solve them in increasingly creative ways.

Dale remembers the pieces of equipment left from when the government official had lived at Cundeelee. He says there was an old scrap heap with lots of neat junk. When the well reached a depth of somewhere around 50 feet, the air became foul - calling for some Yankee ingenuity. Dad found what looked like an old cast iron barbeque, but in reality it was an old forge, the kind a blacksmith would use. (The blacksmith would start the day by building a fire in the coals, and when he needed heat for forging iron would super heat the area by cranking the forge handle activating an air blower. The more he cranked the handle the more air was drawn through the housing that held spinning blades, forcing the air up through the coals.) Dad reasoned that it could just as easily channel that air through a tube down to where the person on the pick and shovel were in desperate need of breathable air. The system worked amazingly well as long as there was SOMEONE TURNING THE CRANK HANDLE.

Bob now had the men to turn the crank handle. They could also haul up the buckets of dirt. He had worked with these young men and knew they were hard workers and trustworthy. "Yes," he thought, "this will work!"

Whether he wanted to or not, he was back in the exhausting but crucial groove of digging for H_2O.

The well had become too deep for a ladder, so he had to either climb up the rope, or be pulled up while sitting in the bucket they used to haul up the dirt.

His three aboriginal friends were back taking shifts turning the crank which kept him supplied with the much needed breath of life - that of air.

Up top it was another lovely clear sunny warm day with a whisper of a breeze gently stirring the leaves of the trees, the flies incessantly buzzed around, the birds chattered as they darted here and there, and all else was still.

Soon it would be lunchtime, but for now it was Don at the crank keeping Bob supplied with oxygen while he dug ever deeper. Occasionally Bob would give a holler, as well as a tug on the rope, and Don would stop turning the crank supplying the air long enough to pull up a full bucket of dirt, dump it, and lower the bucket. Bob had learned from experience to keep a watch overhead, for several times the returning bucket had become a downward missile. Words always floated down, after the bucket had landed – sometimes on him, "Ngaru, Tjamu, I forgot!"

However, today things were going well.

Don had once again gently lowered an empty bucket; Bob had gone back to digging.

Someone stopped by to chat with Don distracting him long enough to forget about his job of turning the crank. Finishing their chat under a nearby tree Don sat down, relaxed in its shade and fell sound asleep.

Bob began to feel faint, which he at first ignored and just kept on working, only to feel increasingly ill. It suddenly dawned on him that he was not getting any fresh air and started yanking on the rope and hollering. He became increasingly alarmed when he realized no one was topside. Bob tried to climb up the rope, but to his horror found he was just too weak and collapsed onto the rubble he'd recently loosened. The more foul air he swallowed, the worse he felt. Exhausted by his efforts, he finally collapsed in a heap, while silently offering up a desperate simple prayer for divine intervention.

An individual in need of Uncle Bob's help stopped and woke Don to ask him where Uncle Bob had gone.

Don overwhelmed by guilt, and fear, raced over and began frantically to turn the handle controlling the air, and uncharacteristically loudly calling out "Uncle Bob, Uncle Bob." It seemed like forever before he saw the rope move slightly, but he still had not heard a sound from down below.

People quickly and quietly - almost out of nowhere appeared and gathered around the top of the well.

As usual the men had come armed, for spears were not only used to hunt game; they were also for meeting out swift and sure punishment or justice.

The well was hardly large enough for two people, but in the excitement one fellow, after pulling up the bucket, had them lower him down into the well to help Uncle Bob. Seeing that Bob was alive but weak, he wrapped the rope around him and yelled for them to pull Tjamu up. Then they hauled him up also.

Don knew he had almost killed Tjamu by his neglect and realized that by law he would be severely punished. Raised and poised for action, all spears were pointed right at

81

Don, and the warning rattles of spear shaft vibrating against woomera sounded again and again. As a rattlesnake shakes its rattles in warning of an impending strike, so to these sounds preceded the action of retribution.

Tribal law says, "You do the deed you reap the consequences." Don had "chosen" to lie down and go to sleep. Now justice would be swift and sure.

Bob weakly raised his hand and shook his head, but the spears remained raised and aimed at Don. Summoning strength he didn't know he had, Bob sat up and leaned against the tree they'd put him under to protect him from the hot sun. Pointing with his lower lip in the direction of the headman, while making the sign with his hand for them to sit down, he cleared his throat, and silently prayed for wisdom.

They were not yet ready to sit, and continued to strut, posture, rattle, point and jab tauntingly with their spears in Don's direction.

Bob wanted no blood shed on his behalf. He thought, yet again how interesting it was that these primitive people had many beliefs that were similar to the teachings from the Bible. The Bible frequently refers to a "blood sacrifice" from the Old Testament right through to the New Testament when all was fulfilled and Jesus once for all time shed his blood for our sins. Not knowing this, the Spinifex aborigines have a practice of drawing blood, be it by spear or a stick, before one can be forgiven or a grievance settled.

Bob was up against thousands of years of tribal rituals. He knew it would take a unique solution if blood were not to be shed yet again this day.

His chaotic thoughts clarified and he felt he had been "given" the answer for he knew a possible solution.

The headman had been paying attention to Bob's body language, and knew Bob was now ready to speak. "Nyinakati! Kanmartiwa!" he commanded. Instantly everyone sat down and became silent. They looked expectantly at Tjamu waiting for his response. Uncle Bob or Tjamu, as he was often spoken to using both names, ran his hand lightly over the red dirt in preparation of telling a story. This was the way information was generally shared. [One would never look a guilty person in the eye or shout his or her wrong doings at them, even when preparing to spear someone. A quick glance and away was proper, for to stare was indecent and totally unacceptable behavior.]

Wanting to cool tempers a bit, Bob decided on a long story. Drawing pictures in the soft red dirt, he started with his family, and travels, and how he had come to Cundeelee. He included the reason he had come which was to tell them of Mamakuurti and His Son Jesus who loves them. He continued on and drew a picture of Jesus as a baby, and then of Him dying on the cross with blood dripping down on the ground. Erasing and drawing another picture of Jesus being buried, and then finally he drew an empty tomb.

People started tensing up again when Bob started retelling the events of the day with him in the well and Don asleep under a tree. He told how he had prayed to Mamakuurti while he was in the well, and that truly God had heard and answered.

Some nodded in agreement.

One last time he wiped away the old drawing on the soft red dirt in preparation for the final story. Taking advantage of the hush, he put all of his energies into telling them Don would not go unpunished for by their law that would be wrong. Bob continued with the same crude drawings they understood and as he drew, he talked using short sentences.

Don was going down into the well, and Bob would turn the crank for his air supply until just before the sun went down. The final picture had the sun just above the horizon, a rectangle to signify the well, and a circle with two dots to show a head with eyes peeking over the edge of the hole to show Don coming up out of the well.

When it finally dawned on Don what Uncle Bob's plan meant for him, he jumped to his feet. "No! No!" He implored. "Spear me, but don't put me down in the hole! I will die in that grave!"

Bob tiredly leaned back against the tree, thankfully accepted a cup of extra sugared tea, and waited for the tribal elders to make their decision. If they accepted his suggestion, it would be a radical change for them, as for thousands of years everything had always been resolved only after blood had been shed.

Tjamu had been welcomed into the tribe, and as such was now related in some way or other to everyone in it. Every adult male who was related to an injured party, got to draw the blood of the person who had done the misdeed.

Tjamu was an elder as well as the injured party, so his words today carried great weight.

Time seemed to pass slowly as each elder had their turn at dialogue, gesturing, dirt kicking, and rattling his spears, and then suddenly quietness reigned.

The lack of noise made Bob realize the decision was near, and he opened his eyes to check the principals involved. Spears were no longer pointed at Don, but neither were they at rest, which would be the case if they were leaning up against a tree, instead of still being in the hands of each tribesman.

Don knew he was in a no-win situation, yet still said his choice was to endure the spearing. He well knew that with Uncle Bob being related to everyone, he could expect to be speared at the very least, sixteen times. Don knew if they speared him, they would do it in his thighs, for he had not done this on purpose. Although it would be very painful, he would still be alive. Deep down he just knew he would never live if he had to go down into that deep pit.

Bob finally understood the reason Colin, Stanley and Don had quit in the first place. It was all about fear, stark, heart-stopping, uncontrollable and consuming fear. Don was terrified to go down into a hole that was so high over his head, for in his mind he was going to be buried down there. He just knew he would never come out alive.

The elders spoke and several men grabbed hold of Don, dragging him over to the mouth of the well. He was sweating profusely, his breathing was erratic, and his heart was pounding so that he hardly heard the words his friend Uncle Bob said which were – "Trust me." Don's normally dark complexion was almost gray as he grasped the rope in a death grip before being pushed over the edge. His feet were stuck in the wildly swinging bucket and the men swiftly let out the rope until they heard the sound of the pail hitting the dirt at the bottom and saw the slack in the rope.

For the first couple of hours the bucket was not filled with any dirt as Don shivered, shook, and huddled in one corner deep down at the bottom of the well.

From time to time throughout the afternoon, the elders took turns walking by to check to make sure there were none of Don's footprints at or around the mouth of the hole. Others came by just to call down and chide him, while a few stayed nearby napping and keeping an eye on Uncle Bob to see if he'd stay awake or try to "cheat" Don of air.

Regardless of all of the things Bob could be doing, he sat hour after hour faithfully turning the crank keeping the air flowing down to Don. About a half an hour before the sun set Bob hollered down to Don that it was now time for him to come up. Don was so thankful to escape out of the ground alive that a bond of cement-like trust was created that day between Uncle Bob and Don. They were linked in spirit as lifelong, true, forever friends.

Over the years whenever Don was in camp and not gone walkabout, he and Bob worked together daily; but Don would never go back down into the depths of that cavity in the ground. He had made it out alive once; he would not test fate a second time.

Don had not come straight from the "bush" to Cundeelee. He had worked on a cattle station, lived near town - had been around a bit, learned some English, and absorbed some Australian ways. Not long after the incident at the well, Don caused a different type of uproar when he insisted on two things. He had fallen in love with May, and he wanted Uncle Bob to perform the ceremony.

Tribal elders arranged all marriages according to definite regulations. [If they had run off together, they would have been tracked down and speared as their law demanded.] The elders would have allowed Don and May to marry except for one thing: May had been promised to someone else. To further complicate things not only was she betrothed to someone else, but she was also confirmed to be carrying Don's child. This was a huge transgression and the focus of heated discussions for several weeks.

The missionaries were also caught in the dilemma for Don and May had each professed their faith, and they expected them to live by a higher standard. After listening to lengthy discussions from all three factions (Don, elders, missionaries) Bob "waded in" and took a leading role to negotiate an agreeable solution.

Finally, they were permitted to marry. Don had to provide meat, knives, files and tomahawks to the injured party and his family.

It was the first wedding ceremony performed at Cundeelee. Ethel made sure it was done in style by providing May with a new dress, flowers, a veil and cake afterwards for everyone.

Author's notes:

Information, regarding the location of most watering holes, (rockholes) was a closely guarded secret. Most were small depressions or holes and found in rocky areas, where run off water gathered. They usually held from one to ten gallons of water. There were a few that were larger.

The two so very "promising spots" were labor intensive and ended in frustration, exhaustion, and dry holes - at about 60 and 90 feet.

Water was never located at Cundeelee.

The same lack of water in the 1950's I found had not changed when I again visited the Outback in March 2002.

I was about eight when this event of marriage took place, and can still remember sitting with my aboriginal girlfriends, and of nervously snickering softly behind our hands. It was so foreign to our culture. The new dress, the ceremony, and Mum even picked her some flowers to hold! We girls did not know what we were supposed do or what was required of us. We were getting mixed signals from all of the adults for some were happy, some still upset, others didn't care, and we wondered what response we were suppose to copy. It was the custom to learn by copying behavior. We looked at each other for we were bewildered as to whom to copy and eventually heaved a collective sigh of relief when it was finally all over.

In the end, we figured it was not so bad, because afterwards everyone was treated to a cup of tea and the rare treat - a piece of cake.

It was the story of the year and then almost forgotten, until the year 2002 when I was visiting at Tjuntjuntjara and came face to face with Don and May's granddaughter and great-grandchild.

Even In the year 2003 while some aborigines will work "top side" at a mine, there are still extremely few willing to work in the mineshaft or underground.

Laundry day

Trips & Tales

A salt water creek, soft sand, and much more,
One never knew what the road had in store.

The two vehicles the Mission had at Cundeelee were a very well used Army Ambulance truck, and an old second-hand army jeep and trailer. Although they were definitely not in their prime, they were ideal for the rough terrain. Any lighter vehicle would not have stood up under the work they were given. The truck was mainly used as a transport vehicle and was usually loaded to capacity. At other times the truck was used to haul debarked sandalwood to the nearest railway siding (which was where we picked up our food and water) twenty-six miles south of Cundeelee – at a whistle stop named Zanthus.

The first time Bob saw the road to Cundeelee, he was stunned for it disappeared into the trees. He was expected to follow the faintest of trails - like four-wheeling. The terrain continually changed. Sometimes he was ploughing through deep soft red sand, at other times bouncing on hardpan. He even had to cross a salt creek that had black gumbo hiding just beneath the glistening white crust of hardened salt; and the last stretch to traverse was up a rocky incline. This track had never seen a grader. It was unbelievably hard on occupants and machines alike.

Bob could not continually dodge around obstacles for twenty-six miles and so tried to avoid the biggest and worst problems. The road/track he learned to live with not only had the above mentioned hazards, but also such things to contend with as spiky cactus-like clumps called spinifex. Various other types of small live shrubs live and dead trees, stumps, and animals, had to be avoided.

Talk about bouncing, rock-n-rolling -
The passenger would often rather be out strolling!

By the time Bob navigated the fifty-two miles round trip he was usually stiff, sore, bruised, exhausted - just plain bone-weary.

Dale remembers that one night at the supper table Dad was discouraged over the lack of money - especially for tires. Mum told Dad not to worry. She had been assured while praying that a check to cover the cost of a complete set of new tires was already on its way. She referred to the verse in Isaiah 65:24, "Before they call I will answer; and while they are still speaking I will hear."

At the time, Dale said to himself – "I don't think God is interested in tires. Let's see just how long it takes for Him to answer." In the mailbag, the following week was a letter that read something like, "While praying I felt suddenly constrained to write you a check specifying it is to be used for truck tires. Would you be kind enough to write and tell me what is going on and if tires are needed?"

Bob tried to always take along a person to help him load the water and supplies from the train into the truck, for changing the inevitable flat tire(s), or in case of an accident. This individual was usually an aboriginal man. However, they liked to rotate and not have to go too often for this was not a joy ride. As well as all of the above, it was mostly dusty, dirty, hot, sweaty work.

On the rare occasions when the road was wet, the trip gave new meaning to that four-letter word – WORK. Being bogged was no fun. Many times it was days before all of the supplies made their way back home via the jeep while the stuck truck was abandoned until the mud hardened enough for it to be pulled loose and returned home.

Once in a great while something happened to lighten the tension of making sure the food, mail, and water run was accomplished safely and in the shortest time possible.

Dale relates the following story as Dad told it to us.

One day on the return trip from a "supply run" to Zanthus, Dad was taught a valuable and much needed lesson – to relax and to laugh.

Because of the noise from the engine, his aboriginal companion of the day got his attention by lightly touching his arm. Once he was sure he had Uncle Bob's attention, using his lower lip, he pointed in the direction he wanted Uncle Bob to look, and said, "Marlu." Bob slowed the truck as he looked in the direction indicated, and saw about a hundred yards away, a red kangaroo sleeping under a small scrub bush.

At the top of the rise, Bob eased to a stop and had already grabbed his nearby 310 Greener single-shot rifle, dropped the lever and was preparing to slip in a cartridge, when his companion once again, but this time with firmness touched his arm.

Darting a glance sideways, as was the custom, he saw his friend push out his lower lip and raise his chin in the direction of the kangaroo and in a whisper say, "Uncle Bob, you stay here, only shoot if he gets away from me."

Meat was always needed. Shooting the kangaroo would be quick and sure, and time was precious, but that day for some reason, Bob uncharacteristically said, "Okay."

He settled back in his seat and hoped this would not take too long for he wanted to get home and unload the supplies that were on board. There was always just so much waiting for him to do!

Leaning his head against the back of the seat, Bob closed his eyes. After maybe a minute his eyes opened to check and see if his friend was having any luck and was dismayed to see he'd hardly moved at all. His first thoughts were regarding the time they were wasting, however; his thinking soon changed, from his desires and wants, to observing the drama unfolding before his very eyes.

Bob saw the roo rise from its nap and started to reach for his rifle. A warning signal from the hunter stayed his hand. Now he was an interested party as he watched the aboriginal man mimic the kangaroo's pose until it relaxed and began feeding.

It took almost forty-five minutes for the man to reach his target without startling the animal into flight and then the real fun began.

There was a scattering of trees ringing the center area of an old burn where a fire had cleared several hundred square yards and it was in the center of this "arena" that the following tale unfolded.

The hunter was armed only with his wardi, (a multi-purpose two to three foot long wooden club). The kangaroo on the other hand had his full natural armament: clawed front paws, powerful hind legs ending with toenails the strength of spikes, a muscular thick tail, and wickedly effective big teeth.

The stealthy warrior slowly inched his way toward his quarry from the up-wind side. After what seemed like a lifetime, he pounced on the back of the big red roo. He got in one whack with his wardi (club) before sliding down its back and ended up hanging onto its tail. When the kangaroo tried to get up and balance on its tail in order to deliver a powerful kick, the man would lift up its tail, which in turn knocked the kangaroo off his feet.

Dad said this dance continued for several minutes until his friend, beginning to tire, decided riding would be easier. The Roo gave him the ride of his life – hopping this way and that trying to dislodge him – all the while the fellow kept trying to get a lethal blow to connect. One good blow that should have been the fatal one only made the animal want to fight harder.

The problem for the roo was the gladiator was always behind him. Sliding down yet again the man was hard pressed not to get bounced off, trampled or grabbed and shredded. [If the roo was just once able to grasp the hunter with its front feet, rear back on its strong tail and use its hind legs the hunter would be ripped open from top to bottom.]

At the last second he was able to grasp and hang on to the kangaroo's tail and again control the animal by lifting it each time it attempted to hop. The tail is smooth, heavy, muscular, and hard to hang on to, but hang on he did. The entertaining wild ride went on for about thirty minutes before the situation was resolved in the hunter's favor and without Bob's assistance.

That evening and for many of the story telling evenings to come, if Dad or his friend were present there was no use for any one else to entertain us. We never knew how absolutely true many of the facts were because Dad readily admitted to laughing so hard while watching this spectacle that he could barely see due to the tears running down his face. For the next couple of weeks, each time Dad looked and saw kangaroo meat on his plate he'd be overcome with laughter as he re-lived the scene in his mind.

Laughter is indeed good medicine.

Author's note:

To know our Dad, was to love him, but that is not to say he was without faults. He liked to drive "flat out" - with his pedal to the metal – maybe it was all the years when he had to drive so slowly.

He always liked to be early or "ahead of schedule," accomplish his task, and get on with the next project - in other words – he had to be made to relax.

He was an excellent shot with the rifle – so good in fact, that he was made (not by his choice) an "official game warden" by the Western Australian government. There were a few requirements attached, but the real down side of this title was that he had to stop shooting wild turkeys, which had been a special once-in-while treat.

The above story shows the unique interaction between Bob and the aboriginal people he loved so dearly. Because of the respect he showed them by being willing to stop his busyness they often invited him to share moments in their lives.

Light & Love

The Lord of love came down to call,
With a light so bright, his arm did stall.

For several weeks, there had been a growing sense of tension in the aboriginal camp, which they had chosen to locate down in the valley about a mile away from the missionaries' homes. Tjamu or Uncle Bob, he was called by either name, had not been able to discover the root cause of the problem, as no one would tell him what was wrong.

It was not his culture and asking questions, he had learned, much to his frustration, was not the way it worked. One listened, watched, and then because no one was going to tell him outright what the problem was he hoped he'd make the correct deduction.

Time was running out. Tempers were now flaring much too easily. He knew from past experience that spears would soon fly. Blood would flow yet again unless whatever the situation was could be resolved quickly and to the satisfaction of all.

As superintendent, he had other things to worry about as well: food, water, paper work, the coming visit of government officials, and vehicle repairs. All of these pulled his attention away from the obvious strife brewing in hearts down in the camp.

Another day passed. Nothing had changed. Still no one had told him what the problem was. He noticed wearily that now all of the men had disappeared. He sure hoped they'd gone hunting - just for kangaroo.

The sun was setting when he first heard the "sticks" beginning to talk. All too soon, even though they were over a mile away, he could hear people shouting.

Should he interfere or try to let the situation resolve itself without his intervention. Either way he knew there would probably be bloodshed before the night was over and accordingly alerted Ethel to lay out their medical supplies

95

just in case they were needed for stitching and taping up the resulting wounds.

There was a sudden banging on the Quonset hut's wooden door and there stood Don Sinclair and Colin West panting from their mad dash up from camp.

They gasped, "Uncle Bob, Uncle Bob, come right away. Hurry or she will be killed."

Bob turned quickly and spoke one word loud enough for Ethel to hear - "PRAY". Then he disappeared into the night with the two aboriginal men. He had stepped from a room illuminated by a Tilly lantern into the darkness of night.

His night vision was slow to kick in as he stumbled down the incline. He kept tripping over spinifex and large rocks on the way towards camp. In their excitement, Don and Colin literally grabbed each of his arms, hoisted him up and ran down the hill in the direction of flickering fires and silhouettes of men with spears ready for action.

Bob's heart filled with fear wondering what on earth he could possibly do. Would his presence make things better or worse? He then remembered they had come asking for his help. Bob recalled the Bible verses he'd read so often in the Psalms and especially chapter 121… "My help cometh from the Lord..." and his mind calmed. This fight was not his to conquer – it was God's and whatever the outcome, it was in His hands. After all, He was the creator of heaven and earth.

His eyes darted quickly scanning the scene trying to take in everything and everyone as quickly as possible.

Oh, no, he thought, it involved a domestic squabble and the ramifications multiplied for it no longer was just the husband and wife he had to watch out for but all of the relatives as well, as was their tribal custom.

He saw there were numerous injures already but only one severely injured woman with a nasty gash in her head. He was thankful to see the wound was now just oozing, and not gushing blood, but she still needed immediate attention.

At Bob's sudden appearance, silence reigned for a minute or so - until the women on the sidelines resumed egging-on the men yet again.

As he walked towards the injured woman, Bob noticed uneasily that the individuals who had been near her had gotten up and moved, and all was quiet – much too quiet.

He felt the hairs on his neck and arms rise. Turning, and scanning the area, he saw the woman's husband standing about thirty feet away in the process of arming his spear with its (woomera) catapult.

The people had moved out of harm's way. They were barely visible - just shadowy figures - thanks to their skin color, the darkness of the night, and their small individual campfires.

Abruptly, shouting resumed – that of the people along with the man holding the spear. They were all hollering and motioning for Bob to move away from the woman for the time had come to end it.

It was the way things had been resolved by this primitive Spinifex tribe for thousands of years.

As the man with the weapon backed up some and raised his spear in readiness to start his run in order to throw it with force, Bob, instead of stepping away, stepped right in front of the injured woman. He glanced down at her and then turned. He was facing a barely 5' extremely angry warrior and his 9' spear with its usual nasty barb in place.

At this unexpected development, the warrior hesitated. In the midst of deathly silence, he raised his spear and rattled it several times. Since Bob did not move after hearing the warning rattle the man started his run, and then brought his arm back into its throwing position.

Bob never flinched, kept his eyes on the man, and prayed as he had never prayed before.

The arm was back, all set to release the lethal weapon, when a strange thing happened. It was as if the man's arm froze in position. He even stopped running and after a second or two his arm dropped straight down to his side with his hand still clutching his weapons tightly.

His eyes were staring as if he'd had seen something, but all too soon he began muttering and stomping his feet.

The watching natives were transfixed and eerily silent at the unprecedented scene unfolding before their eyes.

A collective intake of air from the crowd alerted Bob, and sure enough, here the fellow came yet again, running full-tilt and headed right at him with his long wooden spear.

Once again, something seemed to happen just as he started to release the deadly weapon. Instead of launching it, the spear remained in the woomera and locked in his fist.

The aborigines observing this event were mystified, no one had ever witnessed anything like it – no one ever refrained from spearing someone once they started their run! This was unprecedented and they wondered what was causing his strange behavior.

Regardless of the outcome - this was one story that would be told and retold for years to come.

Even though his eyes darted nervously around as if he had seen something that scared him, he was not one to give up easily. Everyone could feel his tension as well as his bewilderment and wondered if he would just walk off into the bush and wait another day for justice to be meted out.

Bob shut his eyes for just a second, took a deep breath, and was thinking of stooping down to help the injured woman, when he heard a noise. Looking up and straightening fast he saw to his horror the warrior was still grimly determined to do some damage and was headed yet again in his direction.

Bob prayed, sweated, and prayed harder as he watched the angry face swiftly closing the distance between them. The man was furious and Bob well knew that angry people are not at their rational best. This time he figured he was a goner for sure and fleetingly wondered why he was not dead already. At the last instant as the spear was being released - it happened – a dramatic and unforeseen change took place.

From being in the path of a rage filled man, and facing certain death from the long wooden spear, Bob saw the rage fade from those same eyes and witnessed them stretch wide open in what appeared to be fear and confusion.

His assailant's arm dropped to his side as if it was too heavy to hold up, then his hand opened, and his weapons fell to the ground. Bob's would-be attacker, now unarmed, turned swiftly and fled merging instantly with the darkness of the night.

A miracle had taken place.

But there was no time to dwell on it. The badly injured woman needed urgent care to stop the flow of blood. Others had many smaller but not life-threatening injuries.

Now that it was over, several of the men helped Bob carry the woman up to where Ethel was still praying and waiting. Once again, she would to do her best to treat their wounds. All she could do for most was to just clean and tape them up.

The woman took priority. Ethel first had to stop the bleeding before she could clean the wound or take a stitch. Her ministering to their physical needs was done without the assistance of any medical experience, advice from a doctor or nurse, or for the patient – the benefit of any form of numbing anesthetic.

While Ethel did the best she could to treat their sores and wounds, exasperation still tugged at her mind over the continuing bloodshed and their lack of any other solution such as mediation.

More than a year passed and other fights had come and gone. One day as Bob and his aboriginal helpers stopped cutting and debarking sandalwood in order to boil the billy for the usual morning tea break, one of the men spoke up. "Tjamu, do you remember the night I almost speared you?"

"Forget?!" He silently reflected that to his dying day he would not forget that experience. How often he'd had nightmares of spears hurtling towards him!

With a small grin to down-play the past tense situation, he said, "u-w-a," drawing out the word, to not only emphasis this word yes, but also to imply for sure, impossible to forget, too right I do, YES!

Eyes downcast the man started drawing and tapping the ground with his finger getting ready to tell his side of the story. "Tjamu," he began, "I was proper wild with you for daring to stand in the way of me spearing my wife. She had been casting looks at someone and I was very angry with her – it was not right. At first I hadn't planned to kill her – just teach her a lesson."

For a bit it looks as if he is becoming worked up, all over again, but when no one spoke, he resumed his story.

"Yes, I was truly proper mad at her. Then I got mad at you too, for there you stood, right in my way, protecting her. At first I thought, if you just saw the spear pointed at you, you would move, so I raised it. Next I rattled it warning you, and still you didn't move so I started to run, and my heart got hard at you, and I decided to spear you, and then my wife after you were dead."

There was a long pause while everyone remembered that night. All that could be heard was the sipping of tea and the birds as they chattered and flitted oh so gracefully through the eucalyptus trees. One did not hurry a story being told.

Fortified by another sip he was ready to proceed. "Tjamu, as I started running towards you, you disappeared and all I saw was bright light and it felt as if a very big hand grabbed my shoulder and I could not move my arm at all.

When I stopped running and started to turn away from you the first time my arm went back to normal again. By the time I got back to my starting point, and turned around, once again I saw you standing in front of my wife.

Too mad to think straight, I headed for you again, determined this time to spear you dead, showing everyone how tough I was and how stupid you were to get in my way." He shook his head, remembering.

"You saw what happened to me the first time, and it happened again the second time, only this time the light was so bright it hurt my eyes, and I thought I would never be able

100

to use my arm again – it was squeezed that hard! But did I give up?"

This time there were chuckles all around and emphatic no's from each of the listeners.

"Tjamu the third time I started for you, I was more scared than mad. I knew something or someone very powerful was protecting you, but for my honor (pride) sake, I was going to try one final time to kill you.

The last time I lifted my spear and ran at you, I tried to close my eyes to the light, but I could not. I saw you standing in the middle of it. Once again, the darkness of night disappeared from where you were standing and there was only bright light – like the sun – all around you until this time I could no longer see you.

This time instead of a grip like steel on my arm, I suddenly had nothing but weakness - no strength to even hold my weapons and you saw me drop them and run away.

I have listened to you telling us about Mamakuurti who loved us and sent his Son to die for us and give us peace of heart. I know that it was the good God's Spirit who was protecting you that night, and that it was He, who sent you to us. I want to walk with the powerful Mamakuurti from now on."

Author's notes:

Dad had not seen any light that night. All he'd seen was an angry man headed for him with a deadly weapon in his hand and murder in his heart.

Mum learned not to be squeamish and became quite adept at quickly sewing things up or back in place. In those early years, I know of two times she had to sew a digit back on a hand. Each time they had been working alone and had to walk over a mile for help.

It was definitely and often a blood, sweat, and tears kind of work – both physically and spiritually.

Because of Dad and Mum's choice to obey and go where the Holy Spirit of God led them, on that day they were privileged to see God at work enlightening the previously darkened hearts and minds of these once primitive Spinifex aborigines.

Dad and Mum believed God's love manifested itself best in and through human bodies/servants. To them it was not about churches, and numbers, color, language or where one served, but all about sharing the Good News of a loving Savior and of His glorious peace.

Kids & Kitchen

Little ones with special needs -
No big acts just kids to feed.

The country was in a severe drought with waterholes drying up, as was the vegetation. Brush fires raged unchecked. Animals once plentiful became hard to find.

Some of the primitive nomads had walked hundreds of miles south until they came to the east/west railway line. Now in strange territory, they were starving and their young were sick, suffering and dying.

They watched other aborigines beg for food from rail travelers. Not understanding picture taking, but learning it did not hurt to have a black thing pointed at you, some traded "photo-ops" for food. They soon learned that surrendering one of their wooden artifacts would obtain an even larger supply of food.

One mother, in an effort to save her son's life, was still breast-feeding and carrying the frail eight-year-old who could barely walk. To conserve his energy and prolong his life, each day as she hunted for food he went along as well – on her back. Word spread from one group to another that if you needed medical care, food, or a safe place to live you should go to Cundeelee.

There was a very fine line between assistance versus enabling dependence that Bob and Ethel struggled with in regards to helping to feed the people in camp. The government required that Bob document the few rations they received - each cup of flour, sugar, tea as well as who received a plug of chewing tobacco. Bob sure didn't like it that he was required to give out that last item!

The men could and did work with Bob, learning skills and earning wages, which could be used to buy extra food or tools of which the favorites were files, large knives, wood rasps, and tomahawks.

The women still went hunting each day for tucker such as grubs, tubers, lizards, and whatever else was in season – be it emu eggs or wild pears (karlkurla).

When the mission at Ooldea closed many of the people came west to Cundeelee. One day as Ethel walked outside she stopped in stunned amazement and stared. Some women were unraveling old sweaters and winding the wool into balls. Beside them others including Don's mother, Ruby, were busily crocheting. They proudly held up their almost completed new hats for her to see.

The small white crochet hooks fascinated Ethel for she had never seen anything like them. In response to her questioning gaze, Ruby held up her hook and said "rabbity-bone". Before long men, women, and children alike were proudly wearing the women's handiwork.

The aborigine women from Ooldea had been used to white ways and there had helped with all sorts of work – from cooking to laundry in return for money or food.

One day Ethel relented and gave Rosalie the tub, a bar of soap, the scrub board and an assortment of clothes to wash. While it is true that Rosalie did a great job and the clothes were scrubbed clean, in the process she had used the entire bar of soap. Ethel learned the hard way and in future gave out only a little piece of soap. Being short of water - it was a long time before those clothes were completely free of soap and wearable.

At Cundeelee, there were not many chores for which the women could be paid. There were only a few mission-aries there at any one time, and each did her own cooking. In the early days on Sunday a huge caldron of stew, was prepared for everyone to share along with damper and billy tea.

Children being hungry, - now that was a different story. How can one see children suffering, hear them crying, and not step in to help?

Although money was in short supply the missionaries began ordering and paying for extra milk – both canned and powdered, which they freely gave to every child. To ensure that there was sufficient for all water was added. At times Ethel added a bit of Milo to the milk for a change of flavor, a little extra nourishment, or simply as an unexpected delightful treat.

The mission resisted much pressure from all sides to take the children from their parents. They felt it was important to keep the aborigine family units together and in tact. They knew it would be important if the aboriginal race was to survive and flourish.

They tried to keep the little ones healthy by teaching the mothers baby hygiene. Ethel started with the basics. A bowl of water, changed only twice a morning, was provided so babies could be bathed and their hair washed. This reduced the number of flies from their babies' eyes. She taught them to check for burns and sores. She tried to explain when to bring them to her for medicine. Bronchitis, pneumonia, and diarrhea were feared killers.

After being at Cundeelee for a week or so, the mother with the eight year old came to Bob with a request. "Please take my son and look after him. Your children are healthier than he is." He felt heartbroken at having to say no. He could only give her some milk for the youngster. [One had to be careful, for in this primitive culture if you gave to one then you had to give to everyone.]

After several days, the mother tried again. This time she got Ethel's attention and repeated her request. Again she was turned down, yet was supplied with a little nourishment for the child. Ethel explained to the others that this child was "big time sick". He needed this medicine to make him well.

It tore her heart to have to refuse and yet, if the truth were told, her own youngsters were on skimpy rations. They began the day with just a bowl of porridge – no variety of cold cereal or buttered toast slathered with jam. When her children received a slice of bread it was often plain or lightly spread with Vegemite, and once in a while yummy, sticky, fly-inviting golden syrup. Another rare treat was bread covered in brown sugar with a little bit of water dripped on it in order to dissolve the sugar so it spread easily.

At first the mission board was more horrified to learn that the "crazy" Stewart family was eating corn, which at that time was considered to be pigs' food, than that they were also eating grubs, lizards and kangaroo meat.

Bob and Ethel were troubled over what to do about the children and especially the frail eight year old they'd named Leslie. They prayed much over what would be best for him.

When the persistent and desperate mother came again her husband added his plea for their son to have a chance to live. This time Bob and Ethel answered in the affirmative. They would take Leslie into their home - under certain conditions. He would be treated just like Bob and Ethel's children. If he was bad, he would be punished the same. He would go to school and wear clothes. But they were still his parents. They could visit him anytime or could take him back to camp to live.

They were grateful and watched their son begin to grow strong. There was a "dust up" though the first time Leslie was punished. Everything halted and all parties were called to confer for Leslie had run to camp and complained. The parents each had their say - Leslie had his turn - Bob spoke. Then it was decision time and the vote was not in Leslie's favor.

He returned to the Stewart home feeling abandoned. Soon afterwards, his parents went on a long walkabout. They were secure in the knowledge that Leslie was well cared for. What they would never know were the effects that their long disappearance would have on him.

As lean times persisted, more youngsters were brought up and left for the missionaries to feed and house. It was not very long before the following six aboriginal boys Leslie, Peter, Norman, little Ron, Brian, and Johnny came to live with the Stewart family. [The following aboriginal girls came under the care of the Sopher family: May, Ida, Mary, Alice, Jill, and Maria.]

Due to the drought food continued to be scarce.

Albert Anderson, known to all as Uncle Bert, was a hard working carpenter from Canada, who loved the people and them him. He was instrumental in designing and building several houses at Cundeelee. When his tools were delayed in arriving, he had to make do with what Bob and Albert Sopher were using. At one point, they were cutting up sheets of corrugated iron using an old-fashioned can opener. It was extremely hard on their hands.

Eventually a dormitory was built specifically for the school age boys. A house constructed out of large white rocks was put up for the girls. Being that water was scarce and thus precious, diluted salt water from Goddard's Creek was used in the cement.

By the winter of 1951, a communal kitchen was needed. The "inside" was outside and wide open to the environment. (Like at a picnic area, where a roof is built over a table to shade or protect one from the elements, while eating.) Over time gunny sacks in which potatoes and other food supplies arrived had accumulated.

Someone came up with the bright idea that they could be used to make walls instead of buying costly material. The burlap sacks were opened out and sewn end to end, then stretched lengthwise and anchored to the existing poles. Once that was done "the wall" was whitewashed by using a mixture of water, lime and I believe a bit of cement. Most of the kids took a turn at slapping the white mixture onto the bag walls.

Over the years, Ethel worked at whatever her hands found to do – mostly concerning mothers, hygiene, and the older children.

During their third term from the end of 1962 through 1968, a significant change took place. While on furlough in 1962, the miracle of surgery had restored her hearing. Little did Ethel realize the role her ability to hear would now play in a new area of service.

This new undertaking started innocently enough with Marilyn Anderson, who had been taken in to hospital due to a chronic ear infection, which had resulted in measurable hearing loss. She had been a breast-fed child who had never been further than arms length from her mother when suddenly she was removed from her secure environment. She was expected to eat unfamiliar foods and to use a fork or spoon that even her mother did not know how to use.

Whenever Bob was in town, he would stop at the hospital to visit the aborigines there. It was in this way that he just happened to see Marilyn and the state she was in (rocking and moaning incessantly) and learned she had been in hospital for a year.

He was able to secure her release, but there was a condition to her being discharged. Bob had to agree that the child would not be returned to live in camp where they had only brush shelters and the earth for their bed. It was in this way that Ethel became the caregiver.

The aboriginal life style had good and yet frustrating logic in their culture – they took what life handed them and moved on. Ethel tried to get the child's family to come up and bond, encouraged them to spend time with her, but they had moved on in life and were happy to have Uncle Bob and Auntie Ethel provide for her. It was one less mouth to feed, and they could see her any time they wished.

Ethel was all too soon extremely busy with the smallest of children – the babies. She became swamped with these littlies. As much as Ethel loved hugging them, tending to their needs, watching them bloom and grow into sturdy youngsters, it was a fulltime and exhausting job.

After Marilyn, it was Ian Anderson who had been diagnosed in the hospital as having Celiac disease. He needed wheat, rye and all other grains containing gluten excluded from his diet.

Christopher Hogan was a bush baby that not only had chronic ear discharge and hearing loss, but also very poor muscle-tone. A real puzzle to his parents, he had also been taken to hospital and returned with the proviso that the mission staff would assume his care.

Then in rapid succession came Anthony Hansen and his cousins Louise and Dawn Hogan. The last two had the same father, but their mothers were sisters. Maybe it was the upheaval or change in food and life style from the bush they had come from so recently, but each mother had trouble breast-feeding.

In an effort to save Louise's life and keep her with her mother, Ethel tried to explain and introduced a bottle-feeding program. They, who would never pick up a twig with leaves on it off of the ground to swat at the flies, but break off a fresh one, didn't think about cleaning the nipple after it had rolled in the dirt. The hot sun soured the milk, the dogs chewed the teat off of the bottle, and the little one got ever weaker.

Ethel knew Louise would die of malnutrition unless someone could be found who understood how to prepare a milk formula and would give it to her at regular intervals. Ethel could not, and would not, accept the loss of this little life as just fate, and so her brood grew.

Bob tried to convince the people to feed only the malnourished little ones tinned food, but ran into three problems. The first was making sure the little tins didn't sit in the sun. The second was that the children got the food, because some of the men developed a taste for the meat-flavored foods for toddlers and ate it themselves.

The third problem hadn't anything to do with the food itself, but the container and the way the can was opened. No one had a can opener, but most had or had access to one of the following items - a large sturdy knife, a tomahawk, and/or a file and a rock. The resulting jagged edges made in the lids and edges of the cans during opening inflicted many a cut, for with neither forks nor spoons their fingers became the utensils.

Ethel long remembered one little child in particular – Louise's half-sister, Dawn. She was brought up and left with Auntie Ethel to get better, for she was very sick. For a while, it was touch and go, and then over time her temperature began dropping until it was finally normal. Dawn, as far as they could tell, was physically well, but remained in the nursery under supervision, for she was just not acting right.

Dawn remained lethargic, unconnected, not interested in food or noises going on in or outside.

One day out of desperation for this tiny listless tike in her clean surroundings, Ethel picked Dawn up. Then on a sudden impulse, instead of setting her down after her usual cuddle she took her outside, found a shady spot, and placed her on the ground. After only a few seconds, Ethel was laughing and running to get her camera, for Dawn had suddenly come to life! Ethel said she had let out a huge sigh, hunched over a little and began smoothing the dirt. She looked like a tiny cubby lady preparing to tell a story, for in her culture before a tale is told (drawn), the ground must be prepared by clearing it.

Dawn was so small and had been in a cot and clean environment for a long time - yet her instincts had won the day and her contentment after being placed in her own environment was evident to all. Truly, there is no place like home!

Ethel looked after the six babies 24/7. She single-handedly cooked, fed, bathed, changed, washed clothes, tidied up after and loved these toddlers with special needs.

To cut down on washing nappies (diapers) Ethel sat them on potty-chairs during each meal. It may not have been very hygienic, but it did cut dirty diapers by dozens a day. In the beginning Anthony, Christopher, Dawn, and Louise were too young to walk, but Ian and Marilyn led her a merry chase as they scampered away at every available opportunity.

Scriptures state children are a heritage of the Lord. All too often missionaries are badly conflicted over what to do regarding their offspring's education – especially once they reach a certain age. Bob and Ethel were no different.

In the 1950's and 1960's the accepted thing was once a child turned six, for the parents to send them to a nearby boarding school. Then at the age of twelve or thirteen, it was routine to return the children to their parents' country for their remaining education.

Bob and Ethel decided they would rather their children were home-schooled with correspondence lessons and keep the family together for as long as possible. Darlene, being the oldest, was boarded out in Kalgoorlie for a trial year. However, when they discovered what was taking place brought her back home to Cundeelee.

Bob and Ethel did not know what to do. They wanted to keep their children with them, yet the mission said that during a second term no missionary children over thirteen could remain at Cundeelee.

There were several things that would ultimately help them to decide. First off was their alien status in Australia. Bob and Ethel had permission to be there and work with the aborigines, and Stephen, having been born there, would be welcome to stay. Being only seven when they returned for a second term, he would be allowed to return and live at Cundeelee. What to do about the three older children (especially Dale and Marilyn) was the painful puzzle.

In Australia, the standard practice was to finish high school and then put in two or three years of apprenticeship or career training. Only after that could one apply to a Bible College, for they never accepted any student right out of high school.

Bob and Ethel learned that once their three older children finished high school they would not be allowed to work or study in Australia because they were aliens.

Not knowing what decision to make they even stalled off the inevitable by delaying their furlough for sixteen months. Yet when they left, they still were not sure what they would end up doing. While at home on furlough Bob and Ethel shared a bit of their struggle with Darlene, but only after the three younger ones were sound asleep.

Since she was seven years of age, Darlene had known she was going to be a missionary. Prairie Bible Institute was made to order for her. She loved to read and was old enough to live in the dormitory assigned to high school students. After graduation, she would be permitted to move immediately into the nearby dorm for women attending the Bible School. They even had a summer work program that would allow her to live on campus and not have to relocate for the summer.

The most pressing problem confronting Bob and Ethel regarding the second term was what to do about Dale and Marilyn. They would both be teenagers and whatever they decided would strongly shape their entire future. Neither Dale nor Marilyn found book learning easy, and even if Ethel was not too busy, which of course she was, she did not have the skills or expertise to teach them.

Both of them had become so closely knit into the fabric of the primitive spinifex tribe that they were losing their American identity.

Dale was gifted with an incredible mechanical ability. Marilyn, they could see becoming a teacher.

While at Prairie, they'd seen many missionaries leaving their children for five to seven years – sometimes with another family, and sometimes to live full-time in the dorms. They wondered if they could make such a sacrifice.

After much prayer and many hidden tears, they decided they had to give Dale and Marilyn the opportunity to reach their full potential in an English speaking environment.

They made their decision and stuck to it. They were questioned repeatedly concerning it. Neither Bob's nor Ethel's families were happy. Each thought the other was bringing undo pressure on their family member.

Surprisingly, neither was there support from their mission board. Their decision was questioned by supporting churches, as well as by other missionaries on the field wondering if that was what would be required of them. Australians interpreted their decision as arrogance, as though Australian schools were not good enough. Even some among the primitive tribe wondered if they would need to give up their children if they became Christians.

Bob and Ethel never let anyone see their tears, which were at times a perpetual flood. This led to many judging them harshly; considering them to be hardhearted towards their own flesh and blood.

Those who criticized never knew the agony Bob and Ethel suffered regarding their absent children or, how the mere act of hugging another's child could, if they allowed it, tear their hearts into ribbons.

Author's notes:

I can still remember sticking my hand into the slimy tub of soap that was used for a long time. First, it was scoop out a bit at a time to clean dirty hands. Later when it had hardened, why all that had to be done was to light a fire under it and it jelled.

Where Rosalie had come from there had been no shortage of water; whereas at Cundeelee, it was often a choice between clean clothes or enough drinking water in order to survive for several more days. Needless to say the flies were attracted to the tub.

Mum had grown up in the depression – where nothing had been arbitrarily thrown out. She used to say – "Waste not, want not. Repair, Reuse, Use up, and last of all Replace."

Ethel had two miscarriages during the first term she was at Cundeelee. If only we had had an airstrip that the Royal Flying Doctor Service could have used. During the second term, she hemorrhaged and was flown to Kalgoorlie hospital. Darlene and I were working in Banff when we received a cablegram from Dad. We then had to wait for three days before learning Mum was going to pull through. After the hysterectomy, her health improved greatly.

In 1962, while on furlough in Seattle she had groundbreaking surgery that restored her hearing. New eardrums were formed using tiny grafts from the veins in her arms. This was "the icing on the cake". The people were awed by her new ability to hear them and shortened her name to Lyunku. There was much laugher when they were caught chatting about things, for they often forgot she could now hear everything they were saying.

Her newly acquired hearing was literally a God-sent miracle, a gift, enabling her to work with the babies.

A year after Darlene graduated from Bible School she was asked to consider returning to Cundeelee in order to help Mother with the babies. The nurse left Cundeelee a week after she arrived and Dad dropped the unfilled job of nurse, on her.

Dad was caring for eight teenaged boys as well as doing all the administration that was required of him as the Superintendent of the Aboriginal Community at Cundeelee.

My sister learned when she visited in 1991 that Leslie, the eight year old, had struggled for years with the idea that Uncle Bob had taken him from his mother. Yet the Uncle Bob he had known as a friend and watched over the years didn't seem to do that to other children. Darlene was able to explain to Leslie the circumstances surrounding his coming to live with us. His parents had wanted only the very best for him. The burden he had carried for so long melted away when he knew the truth: he had been loved by his parents, as well as by Uncle Bob and Auntie Ethel.

Leslie became a very effective police aide in Kalgoorlie. He even had a little booklet written about his work as to what the job of an aboriginal aide to the police entailed. He has since passed on. His younger (half) sister Marna Walker Goodwin is becoming a well-known dot painter. [Author holding one of her paintings on next page.]

No place like home - Dawn

Police Aide: Leslie Walker

Painter - Mama - gave to Marilyn (holding)

We come and we go -
Like the seas ebb and flow.
Never making a home -
Across miles, we roam.
Not here for long -
Like the morning dew gone.

A smile or a frown
In this part of town
Goes a long way to tell
Where our treasures do dwell.
Are we sharing Jesus' name-
Or just our own fame?

Are we praising the King of Kings -
Or simply intent on earthly things?
Do we touch heart and hand -
Or just leave tracks in the sand?
Long after we're gone -
Does Christ's fragrance linger on?

Marilyn Stewart

Jerry & Journey

I want to know the Good God,
Before my spirit leaves this sod.

Bob and Ethel Stewart, along with Albert Anderson, had long been deeply burdened for the inland stone-age nomadic Spinifex tribes. They dreamt of sharing with them the good news of the God who loves them.

In the early years of Cundeelee, many of the aboriginal men began requesting that Uncle Bob make an expedition into the interior of Western Australia. They wished for their people to come to Cundeelee and figured - what easier way than for Uncle Bob to go and get them.

After paying for food and water, the missionaries were hard pressed to come up with any extra – even any spending money. Any surplus went for medical supplies. There was no "slush fund" to buy the fuel, food, another radio, tires, water, and such things necessary to undertake what could be up to a month-long trip. Everything they would need for the inland trip they would have to carry with them from water and fuel to car parts and sleeping bags.

Bob checked continually with the government agency of aboriginal affairs who told him repeatedly - there was no one living in those desert areas. After hearing from aborigines such as Toby, Sargent, Long Jack, Dick, Jimmy and others daily reminding him that were people back there, Bob decided they simply had to make the trip a reality.

The missionaries mobilized. They prayed and wrote letters - to the mission board, and to supporters and friends. Months past and in each mailbag new notification arrived from the board of funds earmarked "Inland Trip". Soon they were able to buy a jeep, trailer, fuel, water, tires, sleeping bags and food for this expedition.

Bob made one last attempt to gain the sanction of the Native Welfare Officers. He desired help, information, maps of the area and the clearance to go inland. He wanted their backing to send out a search party for people related to those already at Cundeelee. Were they not responsible for the welfare of aboriginals in Western Australia?

Instead, he was reminded it was a restricted area and that nobody lived out there. Furthermore, he was the superintendent of Cundeelee by their permission and his written permit was to work with the aborigines only at Cundeelee.

They were adamant – he was forbidden to investigate the aborigines' claims. Not only would they not assist him, they absolutely forbade him to search for aborigines. Seeing his determination, they made it clear that if he persisted in this foolhardy venture and something went wrong no search party would be sent out for them.

If he were to find and return with any aboriginal person, the Western Australian government would NOT be liable for their care in any way. The mission board and missionaries would be responsible for every aspect of care (for their food, water, medical etc. etc.) for any person he brought out for the rest of their lives.

The long trip back to Cundeelee was made even longer due to the heaviness of Bob's heart and his dark thoughts regarding the stern warning he had received.

He had begun hearing reports of weird clouds and weapons testing very close to the area in which he had been told the people lived and roamed. The period of when the people would be in a certain area was closing - soon they would have to wait until next year.

He knew they just had to make this trip – NOW!

Trusting his instincts, and before leaving town, he located an army aerial map, picked up extra supplies, and items on his "must have list" which included a short-wave radio. They would need this extra radio in order to communicate with each other. It would be the only lifeline available were something to go drastically wrong. Its call letters were NYS otherwise known as Nine Yoke Sugar.

When the door opened to go inland, as he was still convinced it would, he wanted to be ready to roll.

Upon arriving home, (Cundeelee) Bob went straight to camp to confer with the tribal leaders. He shared the fact that as Superintendent he had been expressly forbidden to go into the interior in search of their relatives.

The government had a large input in the work and he knew as their representative, as well as for the good of the people, in this case he needed to obey their commands. Bob said that without government funding, Cundeelee would not have been able to survive.

He recommended that they consider approving his choice of men to drive the jeep and trailer. He assured them that everything was ready for the trip to get underway. They would need to choose the aboriginal men to be part of the four-man team.

Bob then shared with the missionaries that he had been forbidden to go inland and was looking for volunteers to go in his place. This was a shock. Everyone knew Bob's desperate desire to go, and had expected nothing else.

The last time Albert had been in town a police officer had said something that had stuck in his mind - "No one can actually forbid you to go into the interior."

Albert Anderson had been deeply stirred when he heard Rev. Sopher speak at Biola Alliance Bible College. He remembered, from his childhood days of seeing a picture in the weekly Canadian newspaper. The horror of it, had for all time, imprinted the pictures into his mind. It was a photo of a pile of dead Aborigines with a group of white hunters standing around. The caption was "Catch for the day".

Albert and Roger, a valuable short-term worker, chatted together as well as with the other missionaries and determined this was just the job for them!

"We are going," they firmly announced. "We haven't been forbidden." So it was that the first inland trip was mounted. Everyone rallied to get them ready and on their way as fast as possible.

In a matter of days, the aboriginal guides were chosen and a never to be forgotten adventure inland was under way. The first trip almost ended before it began. A sudden and heavy rain shower had made the rough road very slippery. They got just passed Zanthus when the heavily laden jeep trailer jack-knifed. They limped back to Cundeelee where repairs were made.

Many miles away, and many years in the making, an incredible miracle was about to begin to unfold.

The following is Jerry's story.

I was born in the interior spinifex region of Western Australia, far removed from any culture except my own. My days were occupied tracking and hunting for game such as kangaroos and emus. The women and children foraged for the everyday foods, but it was up to the men of the tribe to find enough meat to completely fill each stomach of our small clan.

We lived from day to day. Sometimes we had plenty to eat and other days and weeks, we just barely survived due to lack of food and water.

I had heard my father and the older tribesmen tell many stories of our past. They told us of Mamakuurti who lives in the sky far above the stars, and of the bad devil that lives in spirits here on earth, influencing us to do wrong. I heard the legend that a long time ago a lot of water covered everything. We have found it hard to think of so much water when we now have so very little.

My people believe that when a person passes on, his spirit can return and live in another living creature, such as their hunting dog. We have many beliefs and fears, which rule our lives. Everything revolves around the bad devil, evil spirits, and witch doctors.

As a young boy, I began to question my elders trying to find out something – anything at all about Mamakuurti. The only thing I had ever heard about Him was from the stories about how He had made the sky, red dirt, plants, animals and us people.

Every time we met up with another tribe during men's affairs (the Law) or corroborees, I would listen for news about Mamakuurti. Each new clan or group we crossed paths with I'd ask my question. Each time I was disappointed to receive the same answer – no one had learned anything more about Mamakuurti. He remained shrouded in mystery.

We have words to tell where He lives and even to explain that He is good all of the time. My heart continually yearned to know how to worship Him properly.

Each new day we focused on surviving to the next. Some years were much harder than others, which was especially true when the rain didn't fall for a long time.

Food was scarce. Tracking down a kangaroo sometimes took days ending with men a long way from the women and children. We would have to walk even further to distant rock-holes in hopes of finding water.

Many years have come and gone and I am no longer in my prime - in fact I am now considered to be a very old man. As a teenager, I went through the rites of manhood. I now have three wives due mainly to the custom of taking and providing for a wife's sister whose husband has passed away. Later I became an elder of the tribe, and even now there is still no news to pass on to the younger ones about Mamakuurti who lives far above the stars.

Every few days we move from one rockhole to the next known water source following game trails and old routes we have used for thousands of years.

One night, now many years ago, for I was a young man at the time, as I lay staring up into the star-filled heavens, my sad heavy heart burst with longing to know about Mamakuurti. The hurt and longing was so deep, this not knowing, that a dam broke inside me and for the first time since I had been a child I found tears running down my cheeks. For several hours afterwards, I lay exhausted, but sleepless due to my emotional break down. Eventually I fell into a deep sleep.

During that night, I had a dream or vision in which I was visited by someone or something hidden inside a bright white light. Words were spoken and a clear and detailed picture of a particular person was shared with me. In the morning I had awakened refreshed, full of energy and in a much brighter frame of mind.

We are normally a very stoic people, but in the morning everyone could tell just by looking at me, that during the night something of great importance had taken place for I was no longer sad.

Stories need their proper setting, time to tell, as well as digest and discuss, so my story would have to wait. Later and hopefully after a successful hunt we would have time for sharing my news. I wanted to hoard the vivid dream/vision to myself, and yet at the same time I wanted to share it with everyone.

That day as always, we began our search for food at daybreak. Our stomachs had not been really full for a long time and so we had begun our years' old ritual of checking for tracks.

All day long the unbelievable, yet oh still so real pictures I had seen during the night, played over and over again with great clarity in my mind. While hunting that day only part of my thoughts focused on following the recently made signs and tracks of several kangaroos. My mind raced yet pondered on the things I had seen and heard during the night hours.

As the day progressed, I began to wonder if there was anything I could do to help make my dream come true. At first I had been thrilled and yet achingly tantalized by the knowledge shared with me. Later that day I began to wonder when it would happen and that thought haunted my every waking hour.

It was from this day forward that I would awake each morning hoping that today my dream would come true, and at night I sorrowed that it hadn't.

Tracking, finding, and killing a couple of kangaroo had come much easier that day and I remember it was almost as if they had come to us. We were happy. This night everyone would be able to have as much meat as they wished. I had believed it was a sign of good things to come.

While the young ones dug a pit, another with long experience, involving the fast rotation of a stick between two hands, created fire. Rocks had been gathered and placed in the hole and a huge hot fire made in its depths.

The fur was singed off each kangaroo, and a slit cut in one leg of each of them. The fire having done its job to heat the rocks had died down. Now it was time to place the kangaroos down into the trench on top of the hot coals. The animals were laid on their backs with their hind legs protruding straight up. The soil was pushed back in covering their bodies.

We left them to bake knowing when the blood spurted out of the slit made in the leg it would mean they were cooked enough and ready to be eaten.

The time had come, while the meat cooked, for me to share my strange story. If I waited any longer I would miss my chance, for we would eat as fast and as much as we could, and then due to such a good feed, fall asleep.

I remember how I had motioned for all to gather close around me and near to my small fire. The young eyed me from the security of their mothers' breasts, while the adolescent boys, not yet men, as was the custom, stayed just out of sight of the women and girls.

I spoke a little louder than usual in order that the gentle breeze whispering through the gum and mulga trees would fly my words to them also. I began by sharing with everyone how I'd fallen asleep looking at the moon and beautiful stars overhead and wishing I knew more about Mamakuurti who lived up there.

Listening quietly they stared, not at me but at the ground or into the flames, as was the custom, and nodded, for this desire of mine was common knowledge.

I thought again of how hard it was back then (and still was) to explain properly what I had seen. All day I had been trying to find some words with which I would be able to describe my vision. I had never seen anything like that which I was about to try to explain and there were simply no words in our language to depict it in great detail and with true accuracy.

Taking a deep slow breath and signaling once again for all to become quiet, I had begun my tale.

"I heard the softest, kindest voice I have ever heard. It said my name and, not recognizing the voice, I opened my eyes to check who it was that was wishing to speak to me.

"It was as if I was looking into the sun, yet it did not burn my eyes, though everywhere I looked was bathed in intense light. I blinked in order to take another look at the shining glistening light and saw an outline as if there was someone standing in the middle of the white glow.

"I heard my name spoken again by that same lovely voice and somehow I knew I was supposed to look in a different direction.

"As I turned my head and looked I was surprised for I saw the strangest of sights and the only things I recognized were the trees and shrubs behind the apparition. There was something tall, which stood upright like a man (or ghost I was not sure) in front of the trees. It did appear to have hands, although they were not the color of any I've ever seen. In its fingers, at about stomach level, it was holding a small black unknown item.

After I had stared at this image for a time, I heard the voice come from out of the light. Yet again, I heard my own aboriginal spirit name spoken. This time it told me about what I was seeing and of things to come. The voice said, "This man you see will tell you about Mamakuurti who lives far above the stars, as told about in the black thing he carries in his hands. Listen well for he will tell you the truth about Mamakuurti and His Son. Truly he will."

"I tell you I took a good long look at this "man" before he faded away, and will try to describe him to you. This man or thing I tell you was white - yes he was - like a ghost with no blood in his face or hands. The rest of his body was hidden or covered. So I don't know if he had any hair, proper arms and legs, or even what his feet looked like."

Taking another deep breath, I had reached out a hand and gently smoothed the red dirt in front of me, for a story was never complete unless accompanied by a drawing. I drew a particular tree in the area (for we all knew the general size of it) followed by "this thing" standing next to it. I explained that yes, "it" really was unusually tall and outlined the shape protruding around his head.

On a different cleared patch I drew his funny shaped nose. With my finger, I drew two lines in the ground – one for each side of his body and ended the sketch with the weird things that anchored him to the ground. They did not look anything like our feet.

At this point in my description and drawing there were muffled murmurs among the crowd followed by each person instinctively fearfully and quickly checking the surrounding area. All seemed normal, but everyone was definitely on edge.

My drawing was not quite complete for I had one more thing to sketch. I now added the small rectangle - telling everyone that it was (maru) or black in color.

For a little while, everyone kept silent as they peered at my drawing, and then I quickly erased it.

(No drawings were ever left "open" for the spirits to see – after a story, they were always quickly erased.)

Fearfully, again and yet still again, we continued checking over our shoulders in quick sharp glances, and moved closer to the warmth of the fire. This was truly a most unbelievable and unsettling story.

Whispered questions and answers were finally interrupted by spurts of blood shooting out of the slits in the legs of our meal - dinner was now ready.

Our next small gathering in this area would not be for at least a year and a big get-together, as this one had been, would not happen for several years or longer. It all depended on the amount of rainfall.

During the remaining few days we were together, I spent much time thinking. Before everyone parted ways, I wished to share my thoughts. I knew I would do almost anything to make my dream become a reality. This particular event in my life had taken place at one of our biggest tribal meetings, and I felt the timing of this dream was important.

The night before we were to go our separate ways, I took the opportunity to tell each group which direction to take. I made sure each small clan took a different route. I reminded each individual that when they found this "white ghost of a man" they were to return here, to this spot, at this time of year. I would be anxiously awaiting their news.

I told them that my family and I would return around this time of the season every year. We would light a signal fire each day to let them know our location, so they would not lose time looking for us. I wished to quickly meet this "white ghost like man" who would tell our people all about Mamakuurti and His Son.

I was young then, and now I am old and feeble.

I kept my promise and year after year, I faithfully returned. Day after day, we lit fires, stayed in the area, scanned the horizon, and hunted until food became critically scarce and the water hole ran dry. We always had to leave in order to survive.

Every time I had returned with high hopes and left close to despair. The years continued to pass and still no one had returned, and I still knew nothing about Mamakuurti. Many more of my people have died, and now this will be my last visit as well. My years are fast running out and my hope, which had been so high, now is almost gone. However, just as I had said I would, I have returned yet again – for the very last time.

We have now been in this area almost too long, but I remained firm - we just HAD to stay a little longer. Yesterday we began heading eastward towards the next rockhole but slower than usual. What possible difference would just one or two extra days here mean in our lives?

They granted my request in that we did not go so far that we could not spot a smoke signal should one occur.

This morning was clear and cloudless and as usual the sky a bright blue. In my mind's eye it was as if I could see forever regardless of the direction in which I looked. In reality, my eyes are infected so that I can hardly see and no longer am I capable of hunting for our meat. I must spend my days foraging with the women and children. My restless blurred gaze wanders at will, seeing my home of red dirt, spinifex, small shrubs, and few trees – this is the land of my tribe from time long past.

This morning when I awoke I was convinced I needed to start a smoky fire. I just knew this was to be my day. The last chance I would have to learn the answer to my life long quest. I would NOT miss it.

A young boy ran over to tell me he has spotted what appears to be a tiny white cloud on the horizon. My heart (or as we would say, "my stomach") responded in joy as another reports it is definitely smoke.

I spurred my small group into further action as I uncharacteristically yell for anyone and everyone to get busy, to light another isolated spinifex clump on fire and bring green branches. I wanted to make sure they saw we were answering. After we lit the fire, I was suddenly afraid it could be a trap of some sort, for this time when we came together; we had heard some very strange tales.

Drawings, strange tracks we've never seen before, and stories of peculiar clouds that start at the ground and fly upward. We had seen no unknown tracks, and no lightening had occurred for a long time. Had man caused this fire? Was this the signal I had waited for so long, or something else?

As we studied the smoke, we noted that the fire was not out of control, but contained. It was also a very smoky fire, made using green foliage, which meant someone definitely wanted us to see it.

My heart was racing for I just KNEW this was to be the day my dream would finally come true and that soon my life long heart's desire would be satisfied.

We began walking towards the smoke. After a while, we lit another fire and when they did the same, we saw we were headed towards each other.

This went on until evening and we were joyful for I knew the next day that I would have my answer. I could barely sleep for excitement and woke just as the sky was lightening.

Before we lit our first signal fire of the day, we heard a strange and fearful sound. In all my years, I had never heard anything like it. The pitch vibrated the ground and the breeze brought a sound like the growl or snarl of a very large and angry beast to our ears.

Sure that the bad devil was mad, we took off running in order to put some space between that spooky spirit/ghost filled place and us. We shook with fear and yet were unbelievably agile jumping over spinifex and small shrubs in our haste to flee the area. No one stopped to erase their tracks, but ran fast to save our lives from the evil ones.

Only later when we were far from that spot did we respond to another smoke signal.

What a day – one that my dream had not prepared me for - except for the whiteness of the men. They not only looked and talked strange, but they had a peculiar odor as well. The sound of that fearful noise from their beast was still ringing in my ears.

At first, we were not too sure Toby and Jimmy were true aborigines, for their shapes were covered, but their faces and footprints were like ours, and they spoke our same dialect. They left the white camp and came to spend the night with us. That night, by the fire, we talked about family members, but mostly about the good God and His Son, and what they knew about Him. We had never talked so much in all our lives.

In between talking, we watched in fascination as Toby and Jimmy made magic. First, they started a fire with only one tiny stick. Next using no seeds, but some white stuff they made food - what they called damper in the coals.

They made water hot, and in a container that did not burn up when you set it in the fire. They warned us not to touch it until it had been away from the coals for a while, but of course, a young lad had to try it. We all checked the burn mark on his finger. Their magic extended to changing water into a strange sweet drink.

The next morning we cautiously neared the other camp. Toby was going to guide them to our water hole at Koolgahbin while Jimmy and the rest of us would meet them there. Two of the more adventurous young boys decided to go with Toby and the strangers.

They were not inside the monster very long when it started to make an awful noise and began to move away from us. It rocked and rolled as it went right over small shrubs and rocks. Just as suddenly as it had started moving it stopped.

Out staggered our two young boys. Holding their stomachs, they tried to distance themselves from "the creature," but instead dropped to their knees where they were violently and repeatedly ill. We raised our spears for surely, "it" must have harmed them in some way, but Jimmy said, "No. It is the strange way that it walks that upsets the stomach."

After a bit, the boys recovered and we headed towards the meeting place at the rockhole. They were there first so had made a fire and a kangaroo was already being cooked. We still stayed a good distance from the strange creature, but took note of its tracks.

Earlier Jimmy had taken off one of his "covering" and put my arms where his had been. It was warm – the wind no longer chilled my bones. He sought out the elderly and as he took something off he would help them to put it on – and our faces registered at first surprise and then pleasure.

He showed us how to take them off when we wanted movement to hunt for food. I had never had anything sit so heavily on my shoulders and rub against my arms, chest and back – it was a strange feeling.

My mind was overwhelmed with all of the events that were so rapidly taking place. I had seen more strange things and magical events in just two days than I had witnessed in my entire lifetime. Jimmy asked me if I would like to try riding in the "strange creature."

I was becoming accustomed to its noise so mustered all of the courage I had to walk over and touch it. Jimmy helped me in and it slowly started moving. It came down hard and hurt my bottom as it "walked" and then all of a sudden the trees started to fly at us. I burrowed down, just like a joey into its mothers pouch, by putting my head down into the hole where my feet had been and my feet up in the air where my head had been. Suddenly all was still and hands helped me to get out and distance myself from it.

Despite all of these distractions, I continued to press Jimmy about information regarding Mamakuurti. Jimmy talked about Him and then said, "If you go with us we will take you to where they talk about Him all of the time."

Jimmy, Toby and the two white men sat and talked for a while and then Jimmy came back to where we were sitting and talked to us of the decisions they were making. The white men, Toby and their machine needed to leave. Jimmy would stay and walk with us if we wished to leave this area to go to where we could hear about Mamakuurti who loves us. The decision was not hard. I had waited all of my life to learn about Him.

The meal of kangaroo gave us strength to walk for several days. We traveled steadily with Jimmy guiding us into foreign territory. Jimmy did the hunting for us and another large meal of meat replenished our fading strength.

On we traveled through sandhills and rocky ground, clay pans and hard dirt, trees and grasslands, ever south and westward. We traveled from sun up to sun down for a week before Jimmy said, "In two days we will be there."

Each night when we rested next to a small fire, Jimmy talked and drew pictures of things we would see. He told us many things, and always answered my questions about Mamakuurti living far above the stars.

We started to see tracks of many kinds including ones of our relatives – so my wives told me in great excitement.

The last twenty some miles Jimmy was constantly saying the name of a person who had recently arrived or departed. Words were beyond me, and I found I could hardly control my emotions now that I was so close to my heart's desire.

Jimmy took good care of us. From a long way off, we could hear many unfamiliar sounds. He left us some distance from the camp while he went to tell certain people we had arrived.

Upon his return, Toby had informed the people as to who had been found and that we were headed towards Cundeelee. Upon arrival, we were assigned an area, near some distant relatives, to occupy. One relative offered us some meat, another some damper and that lovely sweet liquid called tea. It was like arriving at the largest get together I had ever witnessed.

Over the next several days, I saw more people with white skin including children – it was an amazing thing. The children were bare foot and then I knew that they had feet similar to ours; only the big people covered theirs up.

A white woman they called Pina Lyunku, touched my eyes with soft kind hands and put something in them that soothed and eased their burning soreness. She would do this numerous times in the days ahead until my vision, though never completely restored, improved greatly.

There were so many strange new things to think about each day as well as where did I fit into this new society. I even got a new name - Jerry. While I was listening, thinking, and learning, my eyesight was improving.

A few days after we arrived, Sargent (a relative) came and told me that today would be the day to learn about Mamakuurti who loves us. Together we walked to where the people were gathering and sat down in the shade of a tree. I listened intently trying to soak up all the things I heard.

The third time we gathered I could see better than I had in a long time. After they finished what they called, "singing" a tall man I had learned was called "Tjamu" or Uncle Bob walked over near me and stood under a tree.

131

The hair on my neck and arms stood up for he was the man in my dream – the face I had never forgotten. This was exactly as my dream had been – even to the shape and size of the black thing in his hands to the things he wore on his feet.

I remembered the words spoken to me so long ago – "listen well for he speaks the truth about Mamakuurti and His Son." I listened well.

I had heard whispers that there was a man in camp who had been present the evening I shared my vision so many years ago. I struggled with bad thoughts about him for he had never returned to share this news with us. I was deeply troubled in my spirit. Could it be such good news if he had never bothered to come back and tell us?

I asked Sargent to tell Tjamu to come down for I needed to talk with him. Sargent stayed to help me communicate with the white man who treated us as family.

When Tjamu came, he sat on the ground beside me and shared a cup of tea. He tried to pronounce my Wangkai name correctly but it sounded strange. With Sargent interpreting, I told him of my vision – of his face, which I had seen so long ago, of my long wait – of my fading hope. He was awestruck.

I asked questions and waited impatiently for Sargent to speak in our tongue. I asked him to explain again about Mamakuurti and His son Jesus. Suddenly Sargent motioned for Tjamu to wait. He began talking very fast to me. The words just tumbled out – he was my relative. He was the one who had not come back.

I stared at him in disbelief. I had not recognized him for he was now an old man too. With unfamiliar tears running down his cheeks, Sargent expressed his deep sorrow. While I was still in shock and considering what I had learned, he turned away. He spoke at length to Tjamu giving me time to decide on my response.

Would I allow this knowledge to stop me from having the answers to my questions? Did I want to stay mad? No, I decided, I had come this far – nothing would stop me now.

I watched as Sargent lowered his head, closed his eyes and spoke a few words. Raising his head and smiling at Tjamu, he then turned to me and without a word spoken by Tjamu, began telling me the story of Mamakuurti and His Son Jesus.

"They want to make me clean like after a rain shower?" I asked.

"They want me to live with them after I die?

"Truly this is good news!"

I had a question for Tjamu. "Did your father and your father's father know about Mamakuurti who loves us?"

Tjamu nodded and softly said, "Uwa."

"Why did no one come to tell us this good news? We have waited so very long! My relatives didn't even return to share this good news with us, and I am angry that so many died without hearing it."

There was a long period of silence - each one with his own thoughts regarding people and decisions made.

Jerry seemed to come to terms with the past and that nothing about it could be changed. He understood that now he too had a choice and that it was his alone to make.

He abruptly announced – "Tjamu, I want this Jesus to sit in my heart from now on."

Rejoicing was heard in heaven and the outback, for two souls had just made their peace with God.

(The following letter was sent to me by Roger Green in June of 2003. It was the prayer/rejoicing letter, which went out after their safe return from the first inland trip in 1954.)

Cundeelee Mission Station
Private Mail Bag 8
Kalgoorlie, Western Australia

August 1954

LET THE WHOLE EARTH BE FILLED WITH HIS GLORY

By Australian Central Standard time 3 p.m., we crossed the Trans-Continental line at Loongana and headed north.

In the tiny jeep were the four members of the exploratory team. Bert Anderson at the wheel, Roger Green holding tight next to him and wedged in the back seat between the transceiver (short wave radio) and boxes of food were Jimmy Mardi and Toby Jamieson our two native ambassadors who were to prove so valuable later on.

Bumping on the axles, loaded to capacity with petrol, water, food, clothing, spears, sleeping bags etc. the sturdy trailer maintained a firm grip on the bouncing jeep.

On mile after mile we traveled - through sandy desert, mulga and scrub, around salt lakes and clay pan, over sand hills and ridges and treacherous rocks.

God saw us through.

An impossible task lay before us – miles and miles of desert – an occasional tree – a barren waste – golden sand hills – bush grass – spinifex – one gave place to the next – but no natives.

How could we hope to find them in this vast trackless country? If there were natives, only a miracle could lead us to them.

The miracle happened - at 11:20 Friday 30th of July – 155 miles from the Trans-line.

Toby spotted smoke – smoke means fire – and fire means people – our people.

134

The following day we drove into their camp, but scared by the jeep and previous tribal associations with white men – they had fled. Further smoke signals indicated the direction they had taken and by noon, we caught up with them and first personal contact was made by Toby. That evening Toby and Jimmy left us to sleep the night with their people.

What tales were told around the campfire?

What memories were recalled?

What decisions were made? Was Jesus there?

We arranged to meet at Koolgahbin where our desperate water situation could be remedied. Koolgahbin, once the ancient tribal meeting ground for devil worship, for corroborees and for folk lore, a dirty muddy hole in the center of a clay pan, now became the meeting ground for Wangkai and white man – where God was present and where love not lust was displayed.

There were a dozen people, unclothed and uncared for. The absence of girls was conspicuous and we asked ourselves why? Girls cannot fend for themselves and become another mouth to feed. This country gives sparingly for those already living – so girls are in the way – hence no girls.

Jimmy Mardi - dear Jimmy.

How can we express in words Jimmy's reaction to our answered prayers?

It was Jimmy, who capered for joy – his whole being glowing with unrestrained happiness when the smoke was first sighted.

It was Jimmy, who strode off into the dusk with flour sugar and tea safely stowed away in his swag and all resting upon his thin shoulders to walk the nine miles to his people's camp.

It was Jimmy, who led the people to Koolgahbin and when he arrived, he was dressed in trousers having given away his topcoat, pullover, shirt and all but one blanket. What a challenge to us who sat in warmth and comfort.

It was Jimmy, who led the small procession from the wilderness to the Canaan land – a modern Moses – but black.

He endures as seeing Him who is invisible! What a challenge to sacrificial giving and living for the One who loved us and gave Himself for us.

Surely, these people deserve a chance.

Of strong physique and loving character with a high system of etiquette in camp life, they present a picture of human need.

When the people arrive (at Cundeelee) what have we to offer them -

Rations -
Work -
Shelter -
Education -
Friendship -

Nay, more than these!

Why did we go?

- To satisfy our curiosity?
- For adventure?

There is but one answer to both questions – Christ is the answer to human need, yea, to all our needs and theirs.

Roger enclosed the following handwritten note with the letter regarding their trip.

Dear Marilyn,

Next year it will be 50 years since Bert, Toby, Jimmy and myself caused an uproar in the Western Australian Government.

The newspapers said we had found members of the Wangkai people on the firing line (down range) of the Woomera Rocket Range.

That had little to do with the real reason we hazarded our lives to go inland.

Your father for many years had dreamed of someone making that trip – it was his vision to reach the few wandering desert nomads that were out there in nomad land.

Although it was his vision and he was the leader he accepted the team's decision as to who was to go.

Back east (Sydney) the mission was known as the work of the Telfers and of Albert Sopher. Your father lived in the shadow of these men in those days, but he was the faithful, careful mission leader that was there (in a very difficult environment for westerners) day in and day out. Only a Prairie trained graduate could have endured the desert heat and flies!

For the love of Christ constraineth us.....

Author's notes:

Cooking a kangaroo is usually as easy as putting it in the middle of a roaring fire.

Jerry was a real thinker. He had a firm grasp on reality, as well as a sweetness of spirit. One missionary shared with me that she had heard it was the beauty of the moon that first started Jerry wondering and desirous of knowing the creator of such a lovely thing.

Jerry firmly believed and shared with several missionaries that regardless of skin color our need is the same – peace of heart. The only difference is the white race has had a long time to know the way of peace and light while his race has lived in darkness.

Marilyn Stewart

Headed Inland

Jerry

138

Facts & Fiction

The clouds they saw were weird and wild,
Then illness struck both men and child.

This chapter will give the reader a little glimpse as to the climate and general situation regarding the aborigines in the early 1950's and 1960's.

After Bob Stewart had retired in 1983 and was living in Arizona, he was contacted by a lawyer in Australia. They needed information regarding the people, what they had seen, and any possible effects Bob knew about that could possibly be linked to the weapons' testing at Woomera Rocket Range.

Many of Bob Stewart's reports had been marked "classified" and sealed for 30 years. Now a Royal Commission was going to be looking into this period in time. For several months, a lawyer called Bob numerous times on the telephone. Bob was requested to fill out and return pages of answers to questions, as well as respond in more detail by tape recording his answers and clarifying them in writing.

The following chapter is the result of extensive editing of those responses. Bob Stewart made three tape recordings and thirty pages of notes in answer to questions put to him by the lawyer.

The following is a letter written by Bob to the lawyer in which he gives a little bit of history:

"This is in response to your telephone conversation and your correspondence sent September 17th, 1984, and received here September 24th.

I, Robert Stanley Stewart, am a retired missionary and Baptist Minister presently living in Arizona.

In April 1950 I went to Cundeelee in Western Australia to assist in the establishment of a mission for aborigines under the auspices of the Australian Aborigines Evangelical Mission. The mission was to be established on the site of a previous government ration depot. Upon our arrival we found only a Quonset hut, a bare concrete slab, a tiny tin storage shed, and a pit toilet.

Cundeelee was a very primitive outpost and just covered the basics needed to survive. Upgrading and adding buildings and water tanks at Cundeelee took many years of hard work.

We had some W.A. Government financial help, but not a great deal since the Department of Native Affairs was at that time itself, I believe, very short of money.

I became superintendent of Cundeelee Mission in 1952 and remained until October 1968. My association with the Mission was continuous between those years; my only major departures being when I went on furlough to the United States during 1956/1957 and again during 1961/1962."

Although worded in different ways there were nine distinct questions they wanted answered or clarified as well as the role Bob had played.

The Mission's purpose and function;
The Mission's motive for the trips inland;
The time frame and who was back there;
Attitude of the Australian Government in general;
Did the government warn/protect the inhabitants?
Did the government help financially?
Health related issues of the people contacted;
Regarding a Sacred area;
Aborigines who witnessed the "clouds";

In order to make it easier for the reader to follow, the author has taken the liberty of combining the questions and answers into the following categories – mission, government, trips, health, sacred area and clouds.

MISSION

The founding of the Mission had the consent of the W.A. Department of Native Affairs, which wanted to see the establishment of a settlement out away from town. It was always understood that Cundeelee as a mission would remain so only as long as the W.A. government permitted it, and that they could "pull-the-plug" so to speak, at any time.

The existence of the Mission allowed the Department of Native Welfare to move a number of aboriginal people out from Kalgoorlie where there had been a particularly bad epidemic of influenza resulting in the deaths of about 16 aboriginal people. Once the people were moved away from Kalgoorlie and inland to Cundeelee, I believe that only another three lives were lost.

Allowing the mission to exist had other underlying purposes: to keep the aborigines away from Kalgoorlie and to provide an alternative way of life for them. There were aboriginals who had learned to live by begging along the Trans Australian railway line and were living near town under very harsh conditions.

Bob relates that later accusations "that the same aborigines were back in Kalgoorlie begging," were simply not true. There were natives who begged in town, but the mission sought to help the Native Welfare by keeping the people out of Kalgoorlie, and the mission was for the most part was successful. There were aborigines who did go back to begging – but only after the Native Welfare opened up their reserve at Parkeston, 3 miles from Kalgoorlie. This event encouraged some for a variety of reasons to return and live near town.

It took the mission station a long time to get under way with employment due to the conditions and lack of water, but we did get some things going such as cutting and cleaning sandalwood, native artifacts, teaching of mechanics, and so forth.

Regarding the motives behind the various trips made into the interior - clearly stated on the heading of all our literature from 1949 onward was the mission's purpose: "To reach the unreached tribes of Australian Aborigines with the Gospel of Christ". It was also made very clear to Mr. Middleton and Native Welfare by the representatives in December of 1949 and again in April 1950 when Reverend A.J. Sopher and I were in Perth before we proceeded to Cundeelee.

In April 1950, as was stated to Mr. Middleton the Commissioner of Native Welfare, the express purpose of founding a mission station was to make contact with the aborigines.

Two aboriginal brothers, Sargent Kennedy and Long Jack Kennedy, who came to Cundeelee from Kalgoorlie, told us of the existence of the inland nomadic tribes. We wanted to contact these tribes of whom we had been told lived north of the transline and who had no contact with civilization or the gospel of Jesus Christ.

I did go on most of the later trips and we did do it for the health of the people. However, I was concerned primarily with the Gospel of Jesus Christ to a lost humanity and then their physical and other problems.

At NO time did I go there to interfere with their culture nor was it the mission's policy to meddle with their culture, but to share with them the Gospel of Jesus Christ.

GOVERNMENT

Regarding the second question on your paper - did I believe the government took precautions to warn and protect the inhabitants of the general area?

I have read a number of patrol reports compiled by Messrs. Macauley and MacDougall and some other material about the test program in Australia. Speaking generally - it seemed to me at the time of the tests that neither the State nor the Federal Government was inclined to do a great deal about the aboriginal people. At least until there had been some publicity about the matter.

I also felt that the State Government in some way was under the influence of the Federal Government. However as neither government did much to keep us informed as to what was actually happening, certain actions may indeed have been taken without my knowing about it.

In the case of the State Government, my opinion is that their lapse would almost certainly have been a consequence of their lacking men or money at the time whatever might have been their state of knowledge. So far as the latter aspect is concerned, I have no information or knowledge regarding their thinking.

With hindsight, I see now why so many were against our reaching out to those in need in that area. They said there was no one there and when we revealed to them that there were, it put undue pressure on them - because of the atomic testing going on out there.

I do not recall ever having seen any aircraft, military or civil, flying overhead while making an expedition inland. In the area we traveled we never saw surveillance of any kind – be it aircraft, or vehicles and nor were there any warning signs posted.

At no time did the government of W.A. give us any money or vehicles to help us reach these primitive people - before or after the nuclear testing began. I believe it was because they did not have the finances.

Western Australia covers a large area of land, has a significantly smaller population than Eastern Australia, and has the largest population of aborigines. Regardless of the reasons or excuses, the problem remained of primitives being in harm's way, and too close to the Woomera Rocket Range, and in particular the testing area near Maralinga.

I know of only one exception between the years 1950 and 1968. One woman, a baby and a young girl contacted a survey party and conveyed to them that two or three others had perished. We were in contact via our short-wave radio and a rescue party was sent out from Cundeelee and from Kalgoorlie to bring the survivors in to the mission as well as to find and bury the bodies. Jerome went on that trip and he could confirm that two bodies were found. The third body was never found. Several years later, a party from Cundeelee sighted a single set of tracks. The people believed the tracks to have been made by the one lone survivor - a young boy about 14 years of age.

There was no support in helping to bring the people out of the interior even when their disabilities were made known and stated, as in Macauley's reports.

Regarding your eighth question there was never any doubt in my mind that the government policy was to leave the people in the bush, as they were an embarrassment to the administration.

It was only when it was made public that there really were people in the area, when it was assumed there were none, that some wanted an all out effort for something to be done.

I must commend them on the fact that they did do as much as they could do, in light of what they had to work with – few resources and people.

At Cundeelee we did have some contact with the Native Patrol Officers, Mr. MacDougall and Mr. Macauley, and I have read some of the patrol reports later submitted to the authorities by these two men.

I have read Mr. MacDougall's report to Mr. Middleton about the journey that he made from Cundeelee, the report being dated August 15, 1955 and detailing the finding of his investigations after we reported our expedition of 1954.

I am of the opinion that the eastern boundary of the people's movements as described by Mr. MacDougall in his report is inaccurate. The aboriginal people have told me of their journeys extending as far north almost to Giles and they certainly had contact with Ernabella.

As I understand it, there was only a very limited amount of contact with the people in the vicinity of Warburton Ranges. In my experience, there was also a fairly regular movement of normal traffic between Cundeelee and Yalata/Ooldea.

Mr. MacDougall did tell us that he was to be responsible for the area east from Cundeelee. Nevertheless as a precaution, we continued making our own private journeys inland since we knew there were still people out there and in harm's way.

TRIPS

In 1954, we were able to commence our endeavors to contact the nomadic tribes.

The first search and rescue endeavor left from Cundeelee with European staff members, namely Albert Anderson and Roger Green and aboriginal guides Jimmy Mardi and Toby Jamieson. I did not go on that first expedition but I did accompany the majority of those made in succeeding years.

The first route taken ran parallel to the Trans Australian railway line as far as Loongana and then headed north to the area they had been told contact could be made with the nomads. On the first trip into the outback there were thirteen people contacted and brought back to Cundeelee. We reported our findings to the Department of Native Affairs along with our belief that there were still a lot more people out in that vicinity.

As a result, we were in due course visited by the Native Patrol Officer Mr. MacDougall who then, went out to that same area with Frank McCarthy. (Jimmy Mardi went with them, although his name is not included in Mr. MacDougall's report.)

It was my impression that Mr. MacDougall was initially rather skeptical about the continued presence of any people being in the area around Shell Lakes/ Lake Ell. However, after visiting the place himself, he realized the truth of our statements and in my view was afterwards more receptive to our advice.

The missionaries at Cundeelee did not receive any encouragement from the Commonwealth or Western Australian Governments to make these trips to the interior. I think we may have embarrassed the State Government by showing time and again that there were numbers of people living in that area. There was never any doubt in my mind that the State Government policy was to leave the people in the bush.

We never had any Governmental financial assistance to make the trips nor did we receive any provision of motor vehicles. Once in 1960, the Mission did purchase a jeep through the Government stores. [The purchase price as I recall, was in the vicinity of £A1,900.] It was paid for by my wife, Ethel, who had come into a small inheritance, and Lowell Peterson, another member of the mission staff.

With the exception of the 1954 expedition, all of the rest taken by the missionaries followed essentially the same line. They took a rather more direct route on a diagonal from the railway line through Yellow Tail Bore to a point about 90 miles north of Loongana then up to the Shell Lakes/Lake Ell area. On successive trips, we went a little further each time following the water holes.

The Mission Society funded all of the trips with one exception. In about 1958, the aboriginal people at Cundeelee spread a tarpaulin on the ground and everyone tossed in whatever cash they had. The total collected was then handed over to the missionaries with directions to buy fuel and supplies in order to make another inland trip.

The trip we were then able to make, due to their generous donations, turned out to be the one that resulted in the largest group of people being contacted.

I believe the trips had, at all times, the full support of the aboriginal population at Cundeelee. The people may have had dual motives. First off, they did want to assist in bringing their families in to the mission where there they would be assured of having food and water. Secondly, they realized there was something going on out in the desert, which was dangerous and were concerned about the welfare of their families who still roamed out there.

In my experience, there was always a consistent flow of aboriginal people between Cundeelee and Ooldea or Yalata. Their migrating seemed to follow a pattern, which was usually at the beginning of winter or the beginning of summer. Much of it I understood was connected with "the law" and ceremonial business. I was aware that visits were also exchanged as far north as Leonora and there was also contact with Ernabella. The tribes from Cundeelee did quite well at understanding the language spoken at Ernabella.

I did not understand the reason for the closure of Ooldea Mission. There were visitors from Cundeelee at Ooldea when it was closed. As a result, they brought their relatives, who normally resided at Ooldea back with them. They said they preferred to come to Cundeelee rather than go anywhere else.

We constantly checked during each trip we took, between 1954 and 1961, and the only tracks made were of ours and McDougall/Macauley's vehicles, and footprints of the nomadic people. In later years, we saw signs from doggers as well as other vehicles on the edges of the area, not in the interior part - just the Nullabor Plain area. They never penetrated far or into the inland area of sandhills.

We navigated using old army aerial maps we'd picked up in Kalgoorlie at the Mining Registrar's Office.

We put up some warning signs, one 90 miles north of Loongana where we turned north into the desert. Another was posted at a place we called "The Station" because it was listed on the maps as J.R. Smith's station. We also put up a sign about 15 to 18 miles from the first water clay pan of Koolgahbin, which stated, – "waterless and uninhabited area, you go at your own risk – no water beyond here".

We saw no other signs, though some of the aborigines told us they had seen some signs at other water holes, which consisted of a blue X or cross. Upon inquiry I was told the signs had been put up by doggers indicating they had poisoned the water hole and placed bait around it. The people from the interior would not know what those signs meant. That thought continually distressed me.

Therefore, each time we were in that area we kept a sharp lookout to see if there were any indications of vehicles going further inland than our tracks. We also checked extensively to see if anyone was using the same route, we were following. We knew there could be a problem if any of the primitive Spinifex people followed our tracks out to the railway station at Loongana. We did not want them being poisoned from any of the water holes along the way.

Many of the groups we contacted over the years were too large in number to transport via the jeep and trailer or the International, all the way back to Cundeelee. We did however convey some of the people the entire distance to Cundeelee. Our expeditions would comprise of one or two vehicles. The number of aboriginal guides ranged between one and four. It was never an easy trip.

The ill and the elderly were the first ones chosen to ride back in the vehicle and after that if there was space available others were added. Large numbers of them after first contact with us made their own way to Loongana where we had an arrangement with the railways whereby the people would be railed across to Zanthus to be picked up by us.

We always made sure that the groups we had contacted, and who were walking the distance on foot, were accompanied by guides from Cundeelee who knew about and understood the meaning of the blue signs. As an added precaution, we left large tins filled with water as well as flour for damper at various places along the route.

The trips were hard on the vehicles as well as our bodies. I remember one trip in particular for we had even more flat tires than usual.

We had turned and started back towards Cundeelee and were now loaded even heavier due to the added weight of people. We had people crammed in every available spot for I was loath to leave anyone behind.

When we got into the rocky area, the sharp stones cut the fabric of the casings (tires) all to pieces. When we stopped for tea, I checked the tires and was dismayed at what I found. The worst tire had long splits in the rubber measuring 6 – 8 inches in length. We wondered how in the world we were going to be able to keep going and not pinch the tube inside. I said to J., "Hey, I've got a flannel shirt on. Let's cut the tail off of it, and double that piece and put it down in there and put the tube in on top of it, and see if it will get us through a ways."

Boy was that ever of the Lord!

It sure was – it held for another 50 miles before it shredded. By that time, we were finally within range and made a call on the shortwave radio. We asked Ted to come out the 90 or so miles from Cundeelee with as many casings (tires) as he could find. He came out - whereupon we changed the tires with the jeep that he had brought out. With the new casings, we were able to go right on in to Cundeelee where the people were able to get the medical treatment they required.

We did do one inland trip wherein we provided guides and assistance for a wildlife survey party, which included Mr. Bert Main from the W.A. Museum, Jack Cunningham MLC, and others.

HEALTH

On several occasions Mr. Macauley in his reports remarks on the physical condition of different ones - a woman with a broken leg, a girl with a webbed arm, and others. I did not know he was making reports regarding the physical condition of the people. I did notice that he was very inquisitive as to how they looked and took pictures of some of them.

One very helpful report might be the one that Dr. Riseborough of Kalgoorlie, who at that time was also the flying doctor, wrote in a medical journal. I believe it was in the 1961/63 time period when there were 7 aborigines taken into Kalgoorlie and tested extensively by different doctors from different countries.

The doctor told me that he had come to the conclusion that they might be suffering from yaws of the bone, but that there was no known yaws of the bone amongst any aboriginal people of the interior.

I began to be even more concerned for the peoples' safety - especially in the later years. I wanted to ensure that we had all of the people out of the area and that they wouldn't be hunting for food in that dangerous region. I was concerned for their health and safety should there be any fallout from the atomic tests, as well as wanting to reach them with the Gospel.

At the furthest rockhole, we contacted 30 people, but we had had to leave a vehicle back at The Station as we'd burned out the clutch. We were finally able to contact Johnny Pedlar at the mission station and asked him to bring the trailer as well as the International.

Due to their physical condition, I felt we needed to transport many from this group back with us and as quickly as possible. We could not leave them out there to walk the hundreds of miles to Cundeelee.

Mr. Macauley and I had an argument over whether or not the people should be transported in the motor vehicles. I was not asking for assistance to transport the people all the way back to Cundeelee, but only to get them out of the area made up of large sand hills and back to The Station, which was about 37 miles. From there we would be able to handle the numbers of people and deal with the situation a little better.

But he wouldn't do it. He told them they had to walk. There were three children and two adults who were very sick. I said, "Look at the mucous, and they're very hot. They are running a fever. Instead of being the color they ought to be, they're kind of off-purpley color." I paused. "We'll take these five in - these three children and two adults. But we will take them in for medical reasons. They will be okay, because they'll be company for one another. We'll let the others walk in."

He flatly refused. "My policy is never to let aborigines ride on my truck if they can walk." He was really upset.

"Well look, I'm going to declare this in my report when I get in," I replied.

He said, "I'm putting one in too: how you took these people back to Cundeelee."

I said, "That's all right. Why do you think the government built us a hospital and a school if they didn't intend to look after those who need help out in this area?"

He got angry.

I said, "Well, I'd appreciate a ride back to Johnny Pedlar's vehicle where it is waiting for repairs."

I told Jerome: "Walk with the people. Bring them back to Johnny's truck, and when you get there, we will put as many on it as we can. The rest we will allow to walk down. We'll leave you to walk with them to bring them in to Cundeelee."

Jerome was happy about that. He had no objection at all. When we got down to Johnny Pedlar's truck, we were happy to see he'd come out pretty light, with just one drum of petrol and one of water, so he had plenty of room on his 1½ ton International.

I am not sure how many people we got on there: whether it was 14 or 15. It was really loaded down. They did not have swags or things, because they didn't have any blankets, no clothing or anything.

Bob Macauley and Mr. Pennifold did not come back to Cundeelee, but rather turned and went back to the interior and on out to South Australia through the Musgrove Ranges.

My name from then on, as far as the Government was concerned, was mud due to the report Mr. Macauley filed.

This latest group from the interior of Western Australia had some bizarre physical problems and some were really sick. The Royal Flying Doctor came out and took nine from that group to Kalgoorlie to test them for radiation.

I remember there were medical representatives from several different countries some of which were England, Germany, Japan, - all different places. All of whom were very interested in these people.

Katharine Crowley had bones that curved, and were pitted like volcanoes.

Young Irving Jackson had fingers that he could stretch out, and then they would go right back in. They'd be about one and a half inches long. It was just as though he did not have the middle segment of each finger.

Then there were the people with little sores that came up – which the doctor burned off.

I remember only some that went in to hospital - they include Earl Walker, Irving and Bert Jackson. To my knowledge Bert is the only one of those three still living.

It seemed to me as the different groups of people came to us from the interior there was an increasing number of visiting clinics or doctors. Each new group and especially certain individuals in them, upon arrival, was checked again and again and there was no doubt that there were an increasing number of people arriving with malnutrition and/or malformities.

One year I recall blood tests being done. The samples taken were separated by a hand-operated centrifuge and taken away for examination. I did not ever learn the result of the analysis, but from rumors, I believe there were very unusual blood characteristics found in the samples.

In one group that came from the interior there were 6 who were deformed and 25 who were treated for various health problems dealing with malformities.

I said that the precise reasons for the deformities are unknown, and it has been stated that medical opinion favors hereditary disease. However, until the report of the studies on these people is complete it will not be known.

In light of the different ranges in ages of the affected, and that they all came from the area Mr. McDougall said, "if they came from that area they were too close to the tests." It could still be discovered that they were affected by the atomic tests and the fallout.

SACRED GROUND

[On one of the trips there was a very regrettable incident that the lawyer wanted Bob to explain more fully, which he does in the following paragraphs.]

You asked for clarification regarding the inland trip, which was made in June of 1959. The party was made up of three whites, Mr. Macauley, Mr. Ray Pennifold, and me, and one aboriginal named Bernard who acted as our guide.

In 1956, Bernard had of his own free will, chosen to leave the interior and come to Cundeelee. Having left the interior only three years before he was still very familiar with the area we needed to explore. Bernard knew where the rockholes were, the travel patterns the nomads took due to the season of the year, and to top it off was an excellent tracker.

In the report, there should have been a description of a ten-foot circle of small stones obviously positioned with care. Mr. Macauley spun his International four-wheel drive vehicle around and around displacing them.

When I expressed my horror, he replied, "I'm the boss out here and there is no need for these anymore as there are no people out here."

That really bothered me. Bernard had just indicated he had seen footprints - new ones - fresh ones. They were definitely not old. There were people right around us - very close. I was told by Bernard at the time and other folks later confirmed it that nomadic tribes gathered here every few years to arrange their tribal matters: marriages and for other ceremonies.

This group of people said it was the most important of their ceremonial grounds. They were very angry at the destruction of their sacred ground.

That night both Mr. Pennifold and Mr. Macauley slept in the International truck and not on the ground as usual. Their arrogant behavior almost cost us our lives.

One of the men in the party we contacted at that place was Dean who, I was given to understand, was a custodian of the site. Bernard and Dean protected me that night by sleeping, between me and the people we had just contacted.

STRANGE CLOUDS

There are still some people living who remember seeing the black cloud and can describe it, and the other strange clouds they saw as well. A few of them are Toby

Jamieson, Sam and Freddy Hogan, some of the other Hogans, and Roger Jamieson – all of these would be able to refer you to other witnesses.

I recall it being mentioned to me in about 1954 by some of the people who said they had seen a white cloud in the desert somewhere north from Watson which they considered to be an unusual occurrence and thought might have been "Mamu" or an evil spirit. The people who told me may have made the sighting from a train on which they were traveling. They knew that their relatives were still somewhere back there and were very concerned.

Some of the 1959 arrivals told me about another cloud of smoke viewed by them also north from Watson. My main informant was Bernard Pennington - who is now dead. There may be others still at Cundeelee who have some knowledge including Henry Anderson, Tom Underwood, Freddie Hogan, Joanne Anderson, Carlene West, Sam Hogan and Catherine Crawley. Some of the people named may now be dead.

I heard of that sighting before Myrtle and children arrived at Cundeelee. They also spoke of having seen a mysterious cloud while they were still out in the spinifex. They seemed to me to have been very frightened of this phenomenon; since they spoke of it in hushed whispers and described it as "Mamu." By gestures, they indicated to me that what they had seen was in the nature of a cloud of smoke on the ground. It was neither a normal cloud floating in the air nor true smoke rising from the ground – it was very strange in appearance and it frightened them greatly.

The 1959 arrivals spoke of their sighting with some trepidation also. I do not know if they thought it had any effect on them. I do not clearly remember but there may have been a report of some skin itch on the people who were in the smoke.

Bob Stewart also recorded the following story, which speaks for itself in regards to the attitude and resulting repercussions due to the inland trips being undertaken.

We went down to camp to verify the story about a white person being there. Many of the people came up to me and asked, "What government man MacDougall doing here?" He had been down there talking to the aborigines for about 55 minutes.

I said to them, "Well, I wrote to the government and told them there were a lot of people back there where they were testing the atomic bombs. He had said to the government that there was not anyone there because he had been through that area. Now he's in camp checking with the people who have just come out of that same area."

He talked to them, and they talked right back to him, very strong. You know usually they are very timid people, but they talked right up to him. He was rough when he talked to them at first, and then his tone changed and as he got into the jeep, he said: "Hurry up! I've got to go to Kalgoorlie."

I said, "What's wrong?"

MacDougall said, "Well, I learned that I missed a lot of people out there. I have to go to Kalgoorlie, and when I come back, I want one man to go with me. I've got to get provisions from Kalgoorlie and I want one man who knows that area well to go with me."

I gave him Jimmy Mardi, and it was about three weeks before they returned to Cundeelee. This time upon arrival, he did not stop at camp first, but rather came straight to the compound where he sought me out.

Upon finding me he said, "Mr. Stewart, I've got to apologize. I have been a Presbyterian missionary. I have been administrator of Native Welfare. I know the language. But, when I went out into the interior with Jimmy Mardi - the third day out, Jimmy Mardi said to me: "MacDougall, you're not a Christian man."

He said, "You could have flattened me with a feather." I asked him, "What do you mean - I'm not a Christian man?"

Jimmy said, "You never read from that little black book. You never pray before you eat your meals like the missionaries do at Cundeelee." And he was not a Christian, and here he was telling me: "You're not a Christian man."

Then MacDougall said; "Imagine that: I had to be humbled before the Lord by a BLACK man telling me that."

After that, MacDougall was a different man in the sense of how he treated us. He said, "I've got to go back through that area again and check out the people back there."

Well then it started: - the holding up of my letters and not letting them go public for 30 years – until 1983.

Jack Cunningham was a very big help when he went out. He learned where the aborigines roamed and what was going on at the test site. He did not last too long in parliament after that, but he was very interested. Wally Fraser encouraged us and was a big help. More than one store sold us clothes at a very reasonable rate.

This is my statement regarding the things that you have asked. I trust that I have been of help to the commission in this area and when you do go to Cundeelee let, the folks know that we love them and we still are concerned about them. [This is the note on which the tape ended.]

Author's notes:

Jerome was short in stature; extremely accurate with a spear; and a good and true friend to our dad.

While several of the inland trips located no aborigines, most trips did - ranging from eleven to thirty-four persons who had never seen a white person or anything to do with civilization. Many other aborigines walked to the railway line on their own with no help or guidance from anyone. The missionaries seldom had any trouble when they went inland with a couple of aboriginal guides, for they obeyed their guides' every instruction. There was however often trouble with their vehicles.

Ron Smith shared a morsel regarding an inland trip he went on. While crossing a sandhill the timing chain in the old army jeep broke. He spent three days filing away link pins and substituting nails from the 2 Way Radio box to improvise. They left one man whose name he does not recall, to go and make contact with his people – the year was 1957. Ron said they made arrangements to send up smoke signals on their return trip - after returning from Cundeelee where they returned to make permanent repairs to the jeep. On that occasion, Colin West was with Ron. They just made it back to the railway line when they ran out of petrol and were aided by a crew out working on the rails.

On the return trip to retrieve the trailer and go on further in to South Australia, Colin could not go so Johnny West volunteered. He followed the jeep tracks back to the parting point then followed the man's tracks that they had left behind.

There were several instances during the inland trips in which my father and others almost lost their lives due to the attitudes and actions of other white people in the party. Sometimes it was due to arrogance – as in the case of the official deliberately driving over a sacred area. That time even the aboriginal guides were not sure they would be spared. In the morning, they did a lot of negotiating to spare the other two white men's lives.

Another time it was due to fear, for the officials had not believed there was anyone even close and had scoffed saying nobody existed out there. On getting a few feet from their vehicle and finding they were in the middle of a trap with spears pointed at them, they were barely restrained from shooting those they'd come to find.

It seemed to boil down to their preconceived notions, and attitudes. Their lack of understanding of another culture and race was seen in the absence of compassion.

Some changed - some never did.

Many people, such as the lawyer who contacted Dad, worked hard to get information from the aboriginal population about what they had seen and experienced in regards to the "clouds." For the most part the Spinifex aborigines did not grasp the significance of these meetings and therefore did not share a lot of personal knowledge. Meetings were conducted in public places and questions were asked in a way that discouraged the people from divulging their secrets. What? Where? When? Who? Why? and How many? Were questions that flew at them in a seemly never-ending barrage of words.

These queries, put to them in this manner, tended to overwhelm them, for at the same time they were being asked to share information regarding friends and relatives who had passed on. They did NOT talk about people who had passed on. Once in a great while a person might whisper a word or two to a friend, but it was accompanied with a hand cupped next to the ear in order to stop the words from escaping into the air around them. They certainly did not wish to share information regarding their people, and especially not with strangers. Many of them resented the publicity and did not want their photos taken.

Years have passed and many of the old men who walked away from those meetings saying, "Don't take my photo," still do not wish their pictures to be taken. They are only now beginning to realize the political weight their knowledge and words could have had for their people.

At first, there was much talk about flying our Dad or brother to sit in on the hearing in case the Commission wanted more information, but neither was invited to go. In the end, nothing was resolved at the hearing. However, in March of 1986 there was a series of well-written articles published in the newspaper "The Kalgoorlie Miner." A few of the older aborigines told of their families' and others' actual experiences with those strange clouds. They were the stories not shared with the Commission - the violent nosebleeds, terrible headaches, crows falling cooked out of the sky, of eating them, of people getting violently ill, and of death.

Footprints & Fragrance

**Years passed, footprints in the wind long blown,
Yet miles away the fragrance of love had flown.**

In 1993 I, Marilyn, headed back "down under." A tiny bit of the trip is recorded in *Child of the Outback*, but I did not relay the following information and now I know why.

It was to give another dimension to this second book.

I flew into Cairns, then on to Alice Springs, before heading to Perth, Kalgoorlie and to Coonana. I was finally headed homeward after having been away thirty-seven years.

In Alice Springs there were two places I wanted to visit: The School of the Air and Pitchi Richi. Unfortunately, the school was closed due to holidays, but "The Alice Wanderer" was running. I could get off wherever – to ride the camels, at a date farm, shop in town and yes, at Pitchi Richi. This is where the Famous Ricketts Collection of Aboriginal clay sculptures are located.

I wandered down red dirt footpaths admiring one head sculpture after another, but to me it was as if I were looking into the faces of my friends long missed. After walking the trails and soaking up the atmosphere for a while, it was time for some freshly brewed *[1] Billy Tea & Damper liberally spread with golden syrup.

Holding my mug of tea and wedge of damper, I gazed around the small clearing noting that there were three aborigines and about five tourists.

I was becoming more and more at home with the environment and was overwhelmed with how much I'd missed this land and her native people. Making a quick assessment based on my years of living with the Spinifex tribes, I concluded that the three aborigines consisting of two men and one woman were not all from the same tribal group.

Their appearance and stature were vastly different.

[1] Recipes at the back of the book

159

I took in the fact that the man and woman were off to one side as well as the way in which the man was standing between his wife and the other aboriginal man.

While she sat on the ground he stood - and tension radiated from his stance. Trouble was brewing.

Since I was closest to where the tall aboriginal man stood next to a table, I moved in his direction in order to check out what he had on display. I knew by his height, about 5' 8", that this man was obviously not a desert or Spinifex aborigine. He was standing next to a large round table on which lay all of the usual artifacts such as a boomerang, wardi, a shield, as well as the popular didgeridoo (not used by the Spinifex or primitive tribes). Suddenly I spotted what was causing the acute tension.

I could not believe what I was seeing – he was openly displaying "law" sticks for women and children to gaze at and even buy if they wished.

I was appalled and asked him why he would put out these "sacred items"? They were secret men things - didn't he realize the trouble he was causing the other two aborigines, and possibly himself with the tribe?

When I had seen the items, I had closed my eyes and turned away putting my back to the table while I finished speaking with him.

He was a full blood aboriginal, but seemed not to have been raised with the tribal taboos and likely had more white than aboriginal culture and background.

In clear English he replied, "So what? If people want such things, I will sell to them."

That ended our conversation and I set off to go talk to the aboriginal couple about 20 feet away. They were short – maybe 5'2" at most – and I had hopes that they may have known my family, for they appeared to be from inland rather than a coastal tribe.

The sitting woman was dabbing carefully at a canvas. She was in the process of creating a dot painting. The man, as I said, was shielding her from what lay on the table. So I too stood as a shield with my back to the table and was quiet for a time letting them get used to my presence.

I began by commenting on her painting. Then once I had their attention made a slight backwards head movement in the direction of the table of artifacts, to indicate I was about to talk about what was behind us. Upon receiving a covert glance, which showed me they were listening, I asked if that was what was upsetting them. I went on to clarify by asking, "Is your wife having trouble with what that man is showing and selling on the table behind us?"

I saw them react in surprise at my understanding, for they were seeing me as just another curious white person, who was ignorant of their culture and ways.

Long after I had left Cundeelee, I still thought of the aboriginal culture as mine and was just now coming to terms with the fact that I am a white person.

I had never considered the evidence in the mirror, rather had lived these many years by what my roots or heart told me and not what was reality. It is hard to convey the shock and sadness to my soul when the truth finally penetrated.

I felt as if I had lost my inner being.

My heart, continually cried out, "But I'm not white in my culture and thinking. People are only seeing the color of my white skin."

Aborigines, I sadly thought, see me, as white and that I do not belong to them. White people respond to me as one of them, but now it is my turn to think - I do not belong.

These days each time I look in the mirror, the first thing I see is not my hair or eyes, but the undeniable whiteness of my skin.

It took a few seconds for them to grasp that I really did know and understand what was taking place, and the problem it was for them to even be in such close proximity.

Uncharacteristically vocal, the man began giving me an earful regarding how truly angry his wife was. They both were well aware that she could be speared if she were to get even a glimpse of some of the nearby items that were being displayed so openly.

I heard her mutter threats of having the man speared for what he was so irresponsibly and unconcernedly selling. Her husband was keeping a watchful eye on each tourist who bought an item from that table, who then walked over to see what his wife was painting. He realized they could so innocently bring disaster to her if he was not vigilant.

She was extremely jumpy and nervous about even being in such close proximity to such objects. She had a right to be there, but was sitting about as far away as one could, and still be available to the tourists, who might buy her paintings so they could eat well tonight. They were furious, and in my opinion, rightfully so.

Then I felt their curiosity as to why my mannerisms matched theirs and how I knew what I knew. It was time to explain myself for they would not ask me such an impertinent question – it was just not done.

Glancing quickly in their direction and away, I saw they were open for more conversation. "I am Marilyn, child of Tjamu and Lyunku – Bob and Ethel Stewart - sister of Stephen. I lived at Cundeelee many years ago." I now queried them gently. Had they ever been to or lived at Cundeelee?

The man replied, "No."

I nodded and after a time of stillness was ready to move away, having figured out how not to pass the taboo items again. I glimpsed movement and realized the man had made up his mind to share something with me.

Ever so softly, he replied, "Never was at Cundeelee - not our walkabout area - heard a lot about it though. They were the ones who came to tell our people of the good God who lives above the stars and that He loves us."

Years after the mission had closed and all activity at Cundeelee had ceased, the fragrance of Christ had flown on to other parts of Australia via aboriginal feet.

YES!!!!!!!   I just could not stop smiling.

162

The date was February 28, 2003 and I was chatting on line with my brother Stephen when he shared the following story that had taken place just that week.

A member of the Western Australian government who works in aboriginal affairs had purposely stopped in at Coonana to look him up.
Upon coming face-to-face with Stephen he had said – "You are Bob Stewart's son!"
Stephen said he was not sure if he wanted to praise or penalize him because of it, so Stephen just said, "Yes" and stood silent as he waited to hear the words the man had deliberately sought him out to relay.
The government agent stood still for a bit. Then shaking his head in baffled astonishment over what he had discovered, shared the following. "I have just finished traveling throughout Warburton and the Central Australian Desert communities. Your folks, your dad, Bob Stewart is still very highly revered all through this area by the aborigines!"

The official was totally perplexed by his findings!

Don't you just love it! Definitely a GOD thing!

HALLELUJAH!
HALLELUJAH!
HALLELUJAH!!!!!!!

Author's notes:

Isn't it fun when God uses ordinary individuals – even long after they are gone - to amaze ones in high places! Dad and Mum will never know the impact that their lives and witness had on people. Even to ones they never met and in areas where they never visited or left a single footprint, the fragrance of the love of God has permeated.

From 1950 through 1968, my parents' actual footprints could be seen all around Cundeelee and nearby in the surrounding area – not a big territory at all.

To those who think in terms of churches, buildings and numbers - they would look like failures.

My father had one foot a ½-shoe size smaller than the other, bunions, and severe hammer toes. My mother suffered many years with sciatica running from a heel to a hip plus a very thick and infected toenail. The last nine months of my Dad's life was especially painful. Due to diabetes, the bottoms of both of his feet were red raw open sores and had to be kept bandaged. The doctor wanted to amputate his feet, but due to his having had several heart attacks and one major stroke didn't, for they knew he'd die on the table. He who in the past walked briskly was now reduced to hobbling and as few steps as possible.

Their feet we would say were gross, unappealing, not to be talked about, yet just look at the way God in His Word refers to their feet in Isaiah 52:7 and Romans 10:15... "How beautiful are the feet of those who bring good news!"

What a wonderful thing that God does not see as man does!

Wilbur & Warfare

**Wilbur took for me a blow,
To him I am indebted, this I know.**

Now this story involves a lot of warfare that is true, and while it shows that Bob cared about each individual, it will also reveal their reciprocating love of their Uncle Bob.

The camp had been a beehive of activity for more than a couple of months. Small family groups seemed to disappear over night only to reappear after a couple of weeks. The weather was changing, bringing a hint of fall with cooler nighttime temperatures. It was the season when the lawmakers in the form of many of the older generation, arrived in force. Their duties were to initiate the young men. This included beginning to impart their history, legends, locations of water holes, as well as secrets and information regarding sacred places and artifacts.

There had been several corroborrees and plans made regarding a number of baby girls' future marriage. Some had taken off for a funeral of a loved one who had died. [Missionaries found it disconcerting to be notified by a telegram of an aboriginal person's passing the previous day, only to find upon going to relay the news that the relatives were already on their way to that funeral. It appeared as if they often knew something had transpired before any communication arrived.]

As long as everyone was busy hunting, telling stories at night of where they had been, and whom they had seen, or if they were getting ready to move, life flowed. Tempers frayed and blew far faster when different tribes got together.

They were accustomed to five to fifteen people traveling together where food, firewood, and sanitation was not a problem. Added to that was the combination of different dialects spoken, the presence of several young unmarried women, and having over two hundred people in close quarters which put pressure on everyone.

If a clash started at night and escalated, it would take place in and around their small campfires. This meant the enemy could get very close or even strike without being seen, so major injuries occurred. An added problem was the fire. Most people now wore clothes, but had no idea how flammable they were, therefore fighting at night often added severe burns to the list of injuries. It was during the day, when fighting occurred up where the few mission houses were, that accidents could and often did happen.

Ethel was especially cross when they brought their weapons with them knowing they were going to instigate a fight and were planning to use the mission buildings to shield themselves. On other occasions, the intended victim would come running in the sure knowledge that Uncle Bob would intervene, protect them, and help settle their differences.

Everyone learned to listen before stepping out of a doorway in case a wooden missile had been launched, lest one unwittingly become its victim. Lots of soft chatter was a good thing, beware the unnatural quiet.

His inability to break the cycle of bloodshed as the only way to settle major differences forever frustrated Bob. When the punishment fit the crime, he was not overly concerned about their spearing someone, because he knew they would be speared in the thigh and would soon heal. The small grievances that ended in such unnecessary and appalling bloodshed and destruction tried their souls.

Bob was between a rock, and a hard place. Rather than merely caring for the wounded, he wanted to negotiate lasting peace.

Once when Bob went down to camp he unknowingly became a target by being in the wrong location. An aboriginal named Frank saved Bob's life by his quick action. Although Bob was a good eight inches taller, Frank jumped straight up into the air, shoved Tjamu aside, and took a spear in his thigh. In this way he prevented Bob from being speared in the back.

This near "accident" calmed everyone immediately. Later several of the old men told Uncle Bob they were sorry, but warned him that when their blood was hot they did not see color or the fact that he was white, they only "saw red".

Ever since the night Frank saved his life, whenever he heard the noise of battle, Bob never knew if he should go to camp or just stay out of harm's way until it was over.

With the passing of time, Bob became more adept at sensing when a squall was about to hit and had even been able to diffuse many grievances before they had got totally out of hand.

It was night once again when Bob heard the beginnings of another uproar. Eventually he went down to the camp where he saw a situation in which he figured he could do some good. A woman was sitting slumped over with blood flowing profusely from a gaping wound in her head. Seeing her need of immediate medical attention, he forgot the necessity of keeping his eyes as well as his ears attuned. Single-mindedly he focused only on rescuing her as quickly as possible.

Taking long strides towards her, he swiftly bent to hoist her into a "fireman's lift". However, before he could grasp her, he found himself falling to the ground. He dimly realized he had been pushed or shoved roughly, and the next minute felt the weight of a body fall on top of him.

He was a little bewildered for his head had hit the hard red dirt, and an inert body held him as firmly as if he had been glued to the earth. Soon hands were rescuing him and eyes were covertly checking him over, while he in turn checked to see what or who had landed on him.

Wilbur sat with his head in his hands nursing a swelling lump, a gash, a headache and a severe concussion. He had seen a wardi being flung towards the woman's head. Realizing it was going to hit his beloved Uncle Bob, he reacted with lightning speed to take the blow himself.

It certainly would have killed Bob. Although Wilbur had a very hard head, he still required hospital care. He would never be quite the same again.

Marilyn Stewart

Author's Notes:

In two thousand and two when I was inland at the Aboriginal Community of Tjuntjuntjara, I met up with Wilbur yet once more. How precious to me is this short, stocky, camera shy old man.

On my last day there, my brother took me with him to meet the "flying doctor" plane and I learned Wilbur was to be transported to the hospital in Kalgoorlie. The plane arrived with two people on board which were the pilot and the doctor.

Stephen was there to act as interrupter for Wilbur and his sister for both medical reasons as well as to calm them as neither had been in an airplane. Standing on the sidelines, I watched as the nurse introduced Wilbur to the doctor and added that his sister would be traveling with him.

I could tell the doctor was not happy to have two fearful good-sized adults aboard. His patient would be strapped in a stretcher, prepared for turbulence, but the accompanying passenger – I could almost read his thoughts – "Who knew what she would do in a panic?"

Stephen and I walked over to the truck the nurse had driven and in which Wilbur's sister sat. As Stephen began to talk to her I realized, even with my limited aboriginal vocabulary, that she was NOT going to be forced to go in that "thing" with her brother.

After the doctor had the patient secured he and the pilot walked over to us to say it was time for the sister to board. Stephen, in their presence, again asked her in their dialect if she wanted to go in to the hospital with Wilbur. She rattled off a few words, violently shook her head and made a pushing/shoving away motion to the two men.

Stephen spoke quietly. "She's not going."

"Right, then we're off," they responded. Although they did not say anything else - their body language showed tremendous relief and they made haste to leave as if fearful she might change her mind.

Wilbur continues to have things happen to him.

He had been home from the above trip to hospital for a couple of months when Nancy, an aboriginal woman, passed away. During her stays at Tjuntjuntjara Nancy had loved to sit in a particular spot under one certain tree. After her passing, according to custom, no one was to sit in her spot for a specified period of time.

One day, before the allotted time was up, Wilbur forgot and sat there. Instantly he was in BIG trouble.

Knowing Wilbur had not intentionally offended the people and thus the spirits did not deter Nancy's relatives. They wanted retribution - Wilbur's blood.

For several days, the state of unrest, murmuring and reprisals filled the air. Stephen thought he'd been able to successfully mediate a settlement, for all hostilities had ceased. It lasted for only a day or two before erupting yet again. To most of Nancy's relatives it did not matter, that Wilbur was a little slow in his thinking, or that he had been in hospital for a while.

One day Wilbur's brother, Byron, suddenly took matters into his own hands and publicly speared Wilbur in the thigh. This put an end to the feuding. He actually did his brother a favor. Wilbur, could have been speared by each and every one of the deceased woman's male relatives.

Blood had been shed for the offense. Now according to their culture, forgiveness and healing was possible.

All too often I see myself in their child-like actions – having the last word, a caustic reply, me first, revenge for someone hurting my feelings, and I know that I'm no different in my thoughts and actions.

The fact that the God of the Universe wishes to use my mind, heart, mouth, hands and feet as instruments to show His love to others is scary. It is often hard for me to take hold of and truly understand His ways.

Ah, how I wish we really grasped the idea of forgiveness for sins through the shed blood of Jesus Christ.

I am a sinner who has been saved by God's amazing Grace and love, but each day I have to choose to walk in obedience to His dictates. It is the blood Jesus shed for me that covers me when I confess my sins to Him, and He returns me to a right relationship with God.

"Amazing love!

How can it be that Thou, my God, didst die for me?"

Gospel Recordings - Bible stories

Wonders & Words

**New wonders all around I see,
Believing God's Word changes me.**

Have you ever thought of words, the ability to read or hear and understand their meaning, to be a thing of wonder?

In the early 1950's Cundeelee was visited, independent of each other and for only a few weeks, by Wilf Douglas and Don Richtor. [Wilf was with United Aborigines Mission, and Don was with Gospel Recordings.]

Wilf was a dedicated man and skilled linguist whose heart was burdened for these nomadic primitive tribes. In the 1940's and 1950's while others despised them, he was busy trying to decipher their dialects.

When he came to Cundeelee he spent his days sitting with the people in camp asking one and then another how to say a word, a sentence or a phrase. He would listen and repeat it over and over again until all the people agreed he was using the correct pronunciation.

They could not get over the fact that he was interested in them and in writing their language. Not knowing what that meant they would tell Uncle Bob, "He is one nosy, busy man!"

Wilf told Bob that the Wangkatja dialect had approximately 3000 words – just enough to share what they wanted to say without using any additions. He helped the missionaries understand many words and concepts, which had eluded them.

They already knew from experience that this dialect was short on words to make a sentence. There were no words for - and, if, but, or, the, or even maybe. Only now were they realizing their lack of descriptive words. The words happy, or truly happy, also had to be used in place of wonderful, great, awesome, terrific and so forth.

171

Before leaving Cundeelee, Wilf made two posters. The first drawing was of nine word-pictures enabling the Wangkai people to see their language in print.

The second poster was a story with no written words at all and yet the people identified with the characters. He drew in the Wangkai style showing a broad road filled with aboriginal people on their way to death. He depicted their weapons, their activities, their ways of life, fighting, and how alcohol affects them. They laughed and pointed at individuals identifying their bad behavior from the picture.

On the right side of the paper he drew a narrow path leading to the empty cross. Depicted were a few aboriginals listening to the good news of the Bible and making their way to where the stone was rolled away from the grave. As they knelt, their burdens rolled off. The figures were shown to leap up and smile. As they walked towards God they helped each other. This side of the drawing had no violence – it showed kindness, generosity, and harmony – in other words - peace.

One day after he had been gone for some time, several primers arrived in the mail. These little booklets were made in the same manner with only one difference. On each page there was a drawing of an animal, plant, or item and underneath it not only was the word in Wangkatha, but also in English.

Gospel Recordings sent a person to Cundeelee with a different purpose in mind. Knowing how primitive these tribes were, in that they didn't have a written language, and how long it would take for them to learn to read and write - they made tape recordings in order to produce records to send back for all could hear. He worked from a script.

Once again, hours were spent in camp; only this time after much discussion an aboriginal spoke the given phrase in his own language into the microphone. The first couple of times the tape was played back the people were spooked. There sat Stanley with his mouth closed and yet his words were floating in the air around them.

It took some time for them to calm down, for such a supernatural occurrence was another new wonder of these with white skins. They were fearful that it would rob them of their voice and who knew where it would end up – or worse yet what they could make it say.

It was the words they had heard that would draw them back for it was about Mamakuurti and that He loved them. When the people were not out hunting for food, they sat listening discussing and occasionally vehemently disagreeing with the choice of words for a particular sentence.

One morning the man and his machine which talked back to them in their voice and language, boarded the truck for Zanthus and never returned. Some were afraid he had taken a part of them with him even though they did not feel anything missing.

Months later at a camp meeting, Uncle Bob opened a small box. He took a round flat black thing, laid it on top of a bigger box and turned a small crank like handle. When he stopped winding, out of the box floated Stanley's voice - saying the same things as when the man Don had been there. When the service was over Uncle Bob, after several demonstrations regarding how to make the thing work, gave the box along with the strange flat black items to the elders.

In the weeks and months that followed whenever a missionary went down to camp, they encountered a group listening intently to the words from the Bible. It was so much easier to understand when one heard it spoken by one of them and in their native tongue.

The child later to be known as Carlene Anderson-West was one of the fiercest of bush children. Her tiny but sturdy body housed the wild indomitable tenacity and built-in survival instincts passed down over thousands of years through her Spinifex aboriginal heritage.

She was a true outback child. She had watched, copied, and listened well. Now at the ripe old age of about eight she could, if needed, survive on her own. Despite her outward display of toughness, she was a very bashful and painfully shy young girl. She was shy in regards to people, but very inquisitive in regards to life around her and the activities of her people.

Carlene had helped gather food each day for as long as she could remember. At first it was the seeds from certain grasses that would be ground on a stone until it was a flour-like consistency. Each day she kept busy with the women and other children, hunting for food and at the same time unconsciously absorbing new life lessons.

Already she knew which tree roots could be chewed (then spit out) for moisture, which carried water, or the witchetty grubs, where to find eatable berries, and so on. There were the poison trees to be avoided, as well as snakes, spiders, and scorpions. In this hostile desert region each day came with new, yet ever old, challenges – surviving another day was always the main objective.

Although her tribe did not have a written language or a calendar, which marked the time of year, she had learned about the seasons and the tribe had a routine established. This particular day had started out as a normal family walkabout following game trails and moving towards the next water catchment area known as a rockhole.

Her family had left their location near Koolgahbin days earlier and had met up with others also headed towards Illdune rockhole when they spotted smoke on the horizon. Smoke needed to be investigated, so the fastest and quietest of the warriors hurried on ahead to check it out. Eventually the men returned telling an unbelievably strange tale.

They had come across the most unnatural stationary new animal and had seen many totally new and freshly made tracks on the ground. As they talked, they drew parallel marks on the ground so far apart a man could fit between them. This thing/beast was sitting still. Maybe it was sleeping or dead – for it did not seem to breathe and was completely silent.

They continued their report that some of the other tracks in the sand must have been made by the devil because there was not a distinctive outline of a heel nor could one see any toe marks – just a bit of area filled with funny lines and markings. These tracks or footprints they said were larger as well as further apart than the stride of a normal man. But whatever made the marks seemed to walk on two legs since they could tell the direction in which it walked.

The third startling revelation had to do with who had started the fire.

There were three who seemed to have normal aboriginal faces, hands and feet, although their bodies, if they had any, remained hidden. But it was the other one – the "thing" that was sitting with them, that created the most fear of all. It appeared to be a ghost for it was without color. It/he was sitting and talking to the others but the eyes – What was wrong with his eyes? They were the color of the sky! The nose too was oddly shaped. The warriors had never seen anything like it. In addition, every time it moved, its skin rustled. Furthermore, it had a peculiar and strong scent.

Having imparting this information, they described in great detail the footprints of the three who in some regard appeared to be aborigines.

All eyes were bright with curiosity, as well as fright. It was time for the elders to make a decision to either check things out, or to totally avoid these, as of yet, unexplained and never seen before phenomena.

A plan was formulated. Curiosity would be satisfied, but caution would rule the day. Most of the people would stay out of sight. The warriors would encircle the strange invaders and then bait a trap. Once they were in position, a couple of the women along with several small children were to walk into an open area parallel to the monster's tracks and sit down. Carlene hid in the bushes and watched as the bait was taken.

One of the strangers started to hurry towards the women and children. Instantly he was called back by the other two as well as by the ghost-like creature, which was now standing. [Whew, it was tall!] They had spotted many of

175

the 31 spears pointed at them. Carlene caught the hand signal that the ghost obeyed by returning to a sitting position.

There was much dialogue and shouting as one of the aborigines approached the women and children. After coming within 15 or so feet of them, he laid something on the ground, turned around and went back to the others.

Carlene realized she understood the word he had spoken before he walked away and her mouth watered, for there on the ground was a cooked leg of kangaroo meat. One young man ran from hiding, jabbed the meat with his spear, hoisted it into the air and just as swiftly disappeared. It would be the elders' choice, whether or not to accept the gift by eating the food.

The four by the sleeping monster made a small fire and now she saw more strange sights and smells.

This day changed Carlene's entire destiny. She would remember it for the rest of her life. By that evening, she had her first taste of billy tea and damper. She had seen flour, metal, material/cloth, rubber, a jeep and a strange new species of person – one with white skin. Most important, but at the time she would not realize it, she had seen a book. She had seen the Holy Scriptures that would one day change her life as well as the lives of her people.

That night she sat on the fringes of the crowd listening to the elders talk about family and how they were related to the three aboriginal men. A young boy, later to be given the name, Sandy, on account of his hair color, wiggled his way until he was sitting right next to the white ghost-like creature that had its back resting against the monster.

Without warning the ghost-like creature, referred to as Tjamu, reached toward the boy's head. Instead of lightly touching the child's hair, as he had thoughtlessly tried to do, he found his hand grasped tightly. In an instant, he jerked it back, but not before he had been bitten in the webbing between his thumb and finger.

He had been bitten hard enough to draw blood. Now they knew for sure that he was some kind of a human, since everyone knew a ghost could not bleed.

Oh my - the things she would forever remember:
- the first time they heard the monster roaring and how they all ran away
- the first time they had a ride in it and how sick it made them feel
- the long walk they took and how many turned back as it was foreign territory
- the food in the trees and the tins of water deliberately placed for them
- the first time they were given clothes to wear - and the different ways people tried to put them on (In order for them to board the train they all had to be clothed.)
- their first train trip - on a breezy flat car: the unfamiliar movement, the speed at which everything flew at them, the cinders from the steam engine, the noise, the cold
- their arrival at Cundeelee – and how surprised they were at the number of people there were in the world more than she would normally see in a life-time
- the need to recognize everyone's footprints
- there were so many new things that cut her feet and fingers – like glass and tin

Carlene remembers her first dress was nothing but an aggravation. When she'd sit down it would float around her, which made getting up fast impossible. Instead of being able to gracefully stand and race off, she had to think about where her hands and feet were before moving. When she forgot to check, she found herself either taking a tumble – often into a spiky spinifex clump – or else straining to stand while her hand pushed the dress ever harder into the ground.

During foraging, this dress often caught on shrubs upsetting her natural balance, and was in the way when one needed to "do you know what". There was now a problem of getting too close to the fire. When she put her back to its warmth, she could no longer judge how far away she was from it because her dress blocked its heat. It was not too long before she saw someone who had rolled into the fire during the night and had been badly burned.

Things changed yet again when she went to live with the girls at the mission compound. She hated having to go to school where she didn't understand anything being said. The teacher wanted only English spoken because he did not know her language. She had never seen paper, a pencil, books, or a building let alone a classroom.

Girls who had lived in civilization teased her for she loved to go "bush". Some school days the teasing never seemed to end. It was done so subtly by a couple of the older girls that it was almost indiscernible.

Carlene could bite and scratch effectively, but she always got caught. She remembers hearing Uncle Bob say, "That is truly one bush child – leave her alone!" For her this new way of life was no fun at all.

One day the elders came and talked to Uncle Bob. Carlene was not fitting in at school and was maturing early – she needed to return to camp life. And so, Carlene once again was able to spend her days in the bush foraging for food and put on her dress when she came back to camp.

One thing to come out of her shift from living in the bush was the presence of many available unmarried men. She certainly was a popular and much sought after young lady! Small, cute, fierce, cunning, and wise in the ways of the bush – a definite catch to be sure.

Around the age of twelve or thirteen, Carlene Anderson fell in love with an equally wild young man named Johnny West. There was one problem – she had, as an infant, been promised in marriage to Bernard.

When Johnny and Carlene eloped, they understood that if they returned to Cundeelee, a spearing awaited them. Bernard, a much older man, did something unheard of in their tribe - he gave up his claim to her.

Carlene was now a married woman. Although her physical stature remained the same, as time went on she began to expand her horizons by learning new things.

Before leaving this chapter, I would like to share an example of how hearing the spoken Word in one's own language can have a life-changing impact on a person. I have edited the story about Willy Stewart that was relayed to me by Brian Hadfield – a previous missionary at Cundeelee who now lives in Kalgoorlie.

"I'm Silly Willy, Silly Willy Stewart!" was his quiet clear and unashamedly way of introducing himself.

It was always the same, until the last years of his life.

He was one of those older men that you'd hardly notice and I wondered why they called him "Silly Willy". People would twist their finger around their temple and say 'madpa' or kata kurramarta' – "he's mad." I was not any wiser. Eventually he became one of several men who claimed me as 'Marutju' – brother-in-law. He had married Jessie the widow of Earl Walker, whose daughters are Marna and Marilyn.

Sadly, when alcohol became freely available both he and Jessie became addicted. He was always scolding Jessie and was very jealous of her as is very common in such situations. There were often fights between them. At other times, they seemed to be happily married.

One day my wife Dawn and I were walking across the compound when Jessie waved us over and asked us to pray for Willy. Due to the brevity of words in their dialect, we were largely in the dark as to what was wrong with him or how to pray. But pray we must - Jessie and Willy had their heads bowed.

It was a strange situation to be in, but casting this burden on the Lord I began to pray for Willy. Whatever came to mind came out of my mouth in supplication. I did wonder a bit about how and what I prayed, but then just left it with the Lord.

Up to that time, I had not known Willy to be at all receptive to the things of God. In fact, I seem to recall him as antagonistic. However, from then on either Willy or Jessie would often call out for me to come and pray - particularly for Willy. Whatever had been troubling him ceased. Now when he knew a meeting would be held he would be present.

When Dawn and I first went out to Tjuntjuntjara, in the early 90's, there were very few buildings and we stayed close to the Wangkai camp. In the mornings after breakfast as we sat near our fire, Willy would come over and sit down. He needed no invite. We were family – I was his marutju. He began asking that we read from the Scriptures. We read from the Ernabella translation and made a few comments. He then asked that we pray, and Willy joined in.

One day he asked if he could ride with us the short distance to the community. He got his bundle of spears, stuck them on the roof rack and off we went.

As I slowed to a halt, Willy flung open the door, snatched up his tomahawk, grabbed his spears off of the roof rack and took to Glen, a man with whom he'd had a long-standing feud. Willy brandished his axe and spears furiously at his unarmed enemy. Violent, abusive words poured forth from this man who only minutes before had sat thanking God for His love and forgiveness.

Willy rattled his spear – then began jabbing wildly at his legs and chest. I intervened - shouting, "Marutju! Marutju! I did not bring you down here to kill a man. Just now you were thanking Jesus for dying for you, for all your sins, and here you are trying to kill a man!"

"Munta, Munta!" ("Sorry, sorry!") He spluttered and quickly quieted down. Glen had now raced off to get his own spears while I sat down with Willy. We talked and prayed some more. I think the wind had gone out of things by the time that Glen got back. Life went on peaceably from what I recall.

Months later, with permission from the community, I began to resurrect a 32-foot caravan. As it became livable, Willy came and camped with his dogs under a tree close by. Jessie by this time had died so he was alone. He would come around daily for prayer and Bible reading. Later we purchased a small portable Video-TV set and took it and Christian videos out to Coonana and Tjuntjuntjara. Willy loved it, asking for his favorite ones. His favorite was "The Trial and Crucifixion of Christ" with a Wangkayi voice over. I must say that was a favorite.

Willy would not go without his daily prayer and video. One day I got too busy and left Willy to view a video by himself and off he went when it finished. Next day, he quietly asked to see it again, then leaned across touched my arm and said, "Marutju, pray first, inti?" So from then on, we prayed first and watched afterwards.

I had an external power point and a small shelf on which to place the TV set so more folks could sit and watch it. One very warm night, several people came across to watch videos. We watched two or three that night and Willy sat near to me.

We were watching the Trial and Crucifixion again when Willy leaned towards me and whispered, "Marutju! Ngayulu Mamanyatjarrarringu." I had never heard that term before, but its meaning was powerful. 'Brother in law, I have come to (the state of) being with, or having the Father." It is the closest spontaneous expression to "I am now the Lord's," that I have ever heard.

He began to introduce himself saying, "I am Willy Stewart and from that time on people no longer called him Silly Willy."

He has been three or four years with the Lord now. But, he certainly changed from the man who frequently beat up his wife.

Author's notes:

In my mind's eye I can still see the primers Wilf wrote, and the day they arrived in the mailbag, which Dad brought to school. The first page I saw was of a kangaroo with two words printed in big letters underneath it. I vividly remember pointing to the drawing and saying "Marlu" meaning red kangaroo for I had realized it was not a drawing of a grey kangaroo. The English-speaking teacher showed his shock for instead of identifying anything on the pages in English I used the words in my tribal dialect. He was one unhappy teacher regarding this student of his who neither acted like nor seemed to know that she was white and not aboriginal.

While I was visiting Tjuntjuntjara in March of 2002 Carlene and I spent several days together sitting on the red earth under the shade of a gum tree. From time to time her young grandchild came and joined us to sit and draw in the dirt and chat just as I did some forty-five years ago.

Carlene has regretted choosing to run away from school those many years ago. She never did learn to read and write. Now she is making sure her grandchild faithfully attends school. Carlene has recently been attending the newly constructed Women's Center at Tjuntjuntjara (started in the mid-nineties) which is not far from where she met Uncle Bob so many years ago. [He was the first white man she ever saw.]

When I arrived, she had just made a small cloth bag in which to carry her things, as well as begun a dot painting. Just before I left, Carlene said to me, "I want to learn how to read and I have asked the schoolteacher if she will teach me after hours." I know it will not be easy as she is fifty and is often on the move - going walkabout is still very much a part of their lives. Learning to read will be in English and not her first language.

Willy's story illustrates the need and wonder of the spoken word in one's own language. Now both Willy and Bob Stewart have been given new names and a new home in glory.

"Now faith cometh by hearing, and hearing by the word of God..." Romans 10:17

I'm washable – oh don't you see?
From sin and shame – He'll set me free.
It cost the death of God's only Son -
But through His resurrection won -
Forgiveness for all. – He came to save –
His blood the gift – He freely gave.

Marilyn Stewart

Jimmy

Carlene

Stanley Minning, centre, used of God to help with the translation of the Bible.

Richard & Robert

Love from Heaven to earth came –
How far will we go to share His name?

I was headed towards the ending of this book and wondering how to tie it all together. I had written a poem, but it really was not "working" for me. I still had plenty of time to mull over the last chapter when I received the following letter, which had been written years before by my dad. May you the reader be blessed and challenged by it.

Oct. 9, 1967

Dear Wally,

I am sorry to be so late in sending this to you. Please find enclosed one of several experiences that have taken place in the 13 trips that have been taken from Cundeelee Mission looking for the nomadic tribes of aborigines, who up to our contacting them in this area north of Loongana, had never had contact with white people.

The area is in Western Australia about 165 miles north of Loongana and 75 – 85 miles east.

We left Cundeelee on July 1, 1958 in a 1941 army jeep with four in the party - Dick, Toby, Jack and I.

I was the only white person in the party.

Dick's knowledge of the area beyond where Toby had taken Bert Anderson in 1954 was needed. He was really not fit to make the trip having suffered a slight stroke and only several months before returned from hospital. He felt he must go as he was the only one who knew the way to where his people would be, and he wanted them to hear of Jesus Christ.

The trip was uneventful as we left the transline at Naretha and journeyed east, then slowly north away from the line. The only changes came when stones on the Nullabor Plain gave way to more stones. Then north of Loongana about 85 miles the men became very excited and pointing north said, "Two more days Kurta" (brother) to our people. The track now became more difficult and the scenery much more beautiful. The land was now timbered as well as being covered with saltbush.

I wanted to stop for a drink of tea. But, they were not interested in stopping or eating now, so on we went. Their only comment "no time – we must see the people". But sundown found us still not into the sandhill country which we had to go through to get to where the people were living.

Around the fires that night there was no joking or teasing, it was very silent. The thoughts seemed to be - Where? When? Will we meet them tomorrow?

Only 55 miles and 6 hours after leaving camp, a strange sound made itself heard in the motor as well as the sound of the engine missing. It was only after we had crossed seven or eight sandhills that it became clear that we were not going to reach the people in the jeep and still make it out again. We camped, exhausted from digging out the jeep while crossing the sandhills and from the knowledge that we were going to have to turn back from this camp.

After a time of prayer and talking about the situation, it was decided that 2 would go back and 2 would walk on in, without food and only a ½-gallon billy can of water, to look for the people.

I felt that Dick and I would be going back as none of the others could drive and as Dick was really not fit. After talking for a while longer, I went to sleep only to be awakened about 1 a.m., by a whispering voice.

"Kurta," "Kurta," "Kulila." (Brother, Brother, Listen.) I well knew that voice. "When the sun comes up Jack and I will be gone. You take Toby and go home. Come back in 10 days time."

"No," I said, "Toby and Jack are going - you and I will return, now off to sleep you go. You have been too sick to stay out here. Tell the others where to go. They can find them." With that, I fell back asleep, only to awaken and find two empty spaces where Dick and Jack should have been. There was nothing left for Toby and I but to load up and begin the long hard trip back out with a sputtering, missing jeep.

It was two days before we arrived back at Cundeelee. It was to be longer than 10 days before we would once more see our brothers out in the bush.

Time went by fast as we waited for parts and food in order to return to looking for those for whom Christ has a message of forgiveness of sin, and love.

It was 3 weeks before Toby once more lit a match to a clump of spinifex at Koolgahbin Rockhole and we waited to see if we would get an answer to our smoke signal.

It was a long ten minutes as we prayed and waited. Then suddenly off to the right about 10 to 15 miles - Was that smoke? Yes, it was smoke. But were there any people or just Dick and Jack? We went on for about 5 miles in the jeep then lit another smoke signal. Yes, there was another closer coming in our direction.

This went on for about 3 hours then suddenly about 500 yards from us, we saw a fire and as I stopped, I saw 30 to 40 naked people - men, women and several children. They came on slowly until they were about 100 yards from us, then sat down on the ground and lit a fire.

Toby said, "We give them food, mirrors, beads, now Kurta." He took our gifts out about 50 yards and put them down saying, "The white man wants you to have these."

I was very busy looking for Jack and Dick. I suddenly saw Jack in the middle of them, but could not see Dick anywhere. He came back and I said, "Where's Dick, did you see him?"

"No, I can't see him," he replied.

It was not long before two old men came out caring a wooden bowl. They beckoned us up to them. Only then did I see what they had for us. The meat, kangaroo, still had the blood running out of it. There were goannas, blue tongue lizards, and witchetty grubs. Toby's only words were, "Kurta, eat big or it may go hard for us."

187

It was while Toby ate the kangaroo and I the grubs and lizards that Jack came up to us and I got Toby to ask him where Dick was. "He is very sick over there - we have been carrying him on our backs."

When I first saw Dick, I did not think he could make it back to Cundeelee. He said to me in a whisper – "Kurta, I brought my people. Now you tell them of Jesus Christ. Never mind me – you tell them of Jesus!"

In this group and the one contacted later in the day were a total of 66 persons for whom Christ died.

Dick did return to Cundeelee but had to go into the hospital for six weeks and then returned to Cundeelee where he passed on into HIS Presence in Oct. 1962.

Can I ask you a question?

To this man Jesus Christ meant much. How far have you walked to invite someone to come to Christ this last month/year? Shall we not ask our Lord Jesus to give us a fresh vision of Calvary?

The Lord Bless you Wally.

Yours in His service,

Bob Stewart

Author's notes:

Dad often was heard to say the following – "We have three tongues – two in our shoes and one in our mouth and we need to make sure that all three agree.

We need to walk our talk."

Romans 6:23 is the bad news/good news verse of the Bible.

For the wages of sin is death, but the gift of God is eternal life though Jesus Christ our Lord.

Epilogue & Everyone

Hi there, glad you made it to here,
This is an update on family far and near.

Bob and Ethel little knew they would be called upon to face so many and varied challenges, or the cost in health, wealth, and family togetherness they would pay, due to the choice they made to follow God's leading.

They were often unprepared for the emotional desolation inflicted by family and friends, cultural misunderstandings, daily-unwanted adventures, and seeming unending hardships. Nevertheless, through it all they would find themselves with an inner quiet confidence, peace and joy at being in the center of God's will.

They were not perfect and made their share of mistakes. They were human beings with heartaches, homesickness, loneliness, frustrations, being overwhelmed, confused, and yes often full of fear. Both of them felt so very unqualified for the job God gave to them.

Bob had finished high school, but never graduated from College, while Ethel had only finished grammar school and for the first half of her life could barely hear. These apparent limitations did not prevent them from putting their hearts and souls into doing the best they could each and every day. They learned to take one day at a time, pray much, and trust God to give them love, wisdom, strength, courage, and faith to keep on keeping on.

Late in 1968, Bob and Ethel were notified by letter that the mission board and the staff at Cundeelee were dissatisfied with his leadership style, and concerned about Bob's health. They were requesting his resignation.

This came as a bolt out of the blue to him. He had poured out his life for aborigines and missionaries alike for nineteen years. This was the last straw. There had been heartbreak and joy, struggles and laughter, pain and growth, misunderstandings and enduring love for they were family.

189

What hurt so bad was that neither the missionaries nor the board had come to him or even mentioned that they had problems or concerns relating to him.

Bob assumed this was a vote of no confidence by the board as well as his fellow missionaries; therefore, he would not force himself or his leadership on them any longer. Whenever there were misunderstandings in camp or with mission staff, he had tried to get both parties talking and to resolve their issues. Yet when it came to himself all he had received was a vaguely worded notification, with no specific accusations and no names attached.

He figured it was a done deal for there was no indication in the letter that it was negotiable. He replied with a letter of resignation to the board in Sydney then began the heart-breaking task of winding up his superintendency.

It was the honor the tribe had bestowed on Bob that made the dismissal from Cundeelee even more painful. The Wangkai and Spinifex people/his family were totally confused as to the reason for his sudden abandonment of them. He could not give them an explanation without casting a shadow on the work at Cundeelee, and they [due to their culture] could not ask the forbidden question – Why?

Others had determined that their days of service at Cundeelee were over. A shocked, hurt, and saddened, Bob and Ethel packed with no idea of what their future held, and left Western Australia.

God, however, had not told them that their work in Australia was over.

Stunned and taken-a-back by the news, members of the Queensland branch of the mission prayer group invited the brokenhearted Bob and Ethel to Brisbane. They had a proposition for them to consider which would open a challenging and new door of service.

After hearing them out, Bob and Ethel went to spend the next three months with their daughter, Darlene, and her husband Bob, whom they hadn't seen for two years. [They were pastoring an aboriginal church on Palm Island, which is near Townsville.] For Bob and Ethel this was a much-needed time to relax and regroup - a quiet point in their ministry without responsibilities.

Part of their healing came from meeting their first grandchild and being present for his first birthday. The two Bobs enjoyed fishing together whether for men or for fish. The couples cried, prayed, and talked together – not so much regarding the past, but of future opportunities.

Bob and Ethel had been invited to pastor a tiny (six-member) Baptist church in Cooparoo, Brisbane.

How could they know that their experiences among desert aborigines had uniquely prepared them for the coming fourteen years?

Ethel worried about how they would cope with a city church when their ministry had been with primitive people. Bob would have to learn his way around the city, to drive in traffic, and the fundamentals required of a Baptist minister. Ethel was concerned about her lack of appropriate clothing.

In addition to all of those concerns, they had no money with which to furnish the two-story manse that came with the job. In spite of their misgivings, but with no peace of heart to return to America, and no other options open, they accepted the challenge.

They started visitation and having people in for tea. Ethel loved to be able to hop a bus, go shopping whenever she needed, and to minister to missionaries who were passing through. Ethel had a gift of hospitality so it was not long before they opened their home to teenage brothers whose parents were missionaries in Papua New Guinea. Later there were girls that adopted them as surrogate parents, and their home was always open to passing strangers.

One of the biggest surprises was that there was a deaf group meeting separately in the church basement. He made himself known to them and let them know that he was interested in them. Bob let them know that if/when they needed pastoral care of any kind he would always be available to them. He was not demanding they come upstairs and join the hearing members, but they would always be welcome. Bob encouraged the church to have a strong missions program, and it began to flourish.

During this time, Bob studied the required subjects and was ordained as a Baptist minister. Twenty years after leaving Bible College he finally had "papers" that society requires for affirmation. He had studied long and hard and at last, his peers welcomed him as an equal.

After six years and having seen the church grow to over 100 members, they were invited across the river to Clayfield Baptist. Bob continued taking half-hour religious education classes in nearby high schools. He ministered to elderly parishioners at home or in retirement centers, and became a popular conference speaker.

Despite the comforts of 24-hour electricity, running water, nearby shops and medical services, their hearts remained burdened for the aboriginal people.

Bob and Ethel did not have an easy life, and the cost was often high, but I have heard both of them say, "In eternity, it will have been worth it all." They served a total of 33 years in Australia. Upon retirement in 1983, they moved back to the USA and in particular Arizona.

In 1990, I (Marilyn) was with my father during the final hours of his life. He had lost so much weight in the last several months of his life coping with diabetes, heart problems, and all that go with the ravages they create, that even I could barely recognize him.

His African-American doctor had been on holiday for two weeks, so before she entered his room I warned her that he had really deteriorated and that she might not recognize him. She walked in and I stayed outside.

I could hear him greeting her and asking about her holiday. He listened and picked up on one thing she said and turned it into a question about the after life. Did she know for sure where she would spend eternity? He entreated her not to wait but to make sure - now.

She figured she had too much to lose – maybe later. She came out and leaned up against the wall beside me. With tear-filled eyes she choked out, "I'd never have known him.

192

He is my favorite patient! It won't be many days before we lose him, and I can't stand to think about it."

He was released to come home to die. His spirit was ready to meet his Maker, and he could hardly wait, but he lingered for four more days.

In the last half-hour of his life, three times about ten minutes apart he raised his frail emaciated arms heavenward and urgently said, "Up, Jesus, Up!" and then again, "Up, Jesus, Up!"

It gave me goose bumps, for he sounded like a confident child in the presence of a loving father, secure in that he was going to be picked up.

After the third time his spirit was released, and I see him in my mind's eye – ah the peace, joy, and conviction he imparted to me that night that there is life beyond the grave.

I see him not only worshipping his Savior and Lord, but also hanging out "sitting in the red dirt under a tree" with his aboriginal friends and finally being able to speak their language perfectly.

Four years after Bob died Ethel went to live with daughter Darlene in New Zealand. (The "adventure" Ethel had getting there is told in my book *Child of the Outback*.)

She is still living in New Zealand only now she resides in a lovely nursing home called "Sprott House" in Wellington. When I visited her early in 2002, I was impressed with the workers and the atmosphere they have created. After moving her in, Darlene tried taking Ethel out for a drive, but soon realized she could hardly wait to return "home" and would stop fussing and relax only when they turned into the entrance.

An attendant makes sure she gets to the worship service held at the residence each week, and although Ethel did not recognize me (Marilyn), talk at all, or say my name, she knows the music and the old songs. The pianist says Ethel is better than a metronome at keeping time to the music, and the staff has noticed how she is always brighter in her spirit afterwards.

She has been so very ready to go meet her Maker for many years, yet she is still here. The staff loves her, for she doesn't kick, bite, spit or cuss, but she definitely does know that doors and garden gates are the ways out.

In late 2002, Ethel started having what appeared to be mini strokes. She would lay stiff for a few minutes and be totally unresponsive, but suddenly alert and conscious she would hop up, walk down the corridor and start straightening things. During down times, the attendants will read to her from her well-worn forty-five year old Bible. They are intrigued with the notes she has written in the margins.

In her Bible, on a scrap of yellow paper and written in her hand we found the following words:

"Heaven is the most marvelous place that the wisdom of God could conceive and the power of God could prepare." [Attributed to Harry Rimmer]

In December of 2002 several hours after one of her attacks, she was sitting quietly by herself. It was "tea" time and two of the workers were taking around hot tea and cookies to all of the patients. Stopping to give Ethel hers they were astounded and looked at each other in disbelief – had they really heard her speak? Ethel, looking intently at them had said, "Thank you for all the care and love all of you show us."

Having worked for years with dementia patients, they could hardly believe it. She only made humming noises and had not spoken a complete and meaningful sentence in over a year. Later in the week, she again spoke, and again words of thanks came out of her mouth. Another time she greeted her granddaughters with "Hello ladies!"

Another day after an additional set back she opened her eyes and recognized Darlene sitting by her bed. Mum's face reflected her sorrow at still being here on earth. Darlene didn't know whether to laugh or cry. We are now into December of 2003 and Mum still often knows Darlene and occasionally shares a word.

She is the talk of the facility, and is being used of God where she is, even though she does not realize it. Hearts are being ministered to as they read the scriptures to her and observe her thankful attitude.

One of Bob and Ethel's rewards here on earth was in having friends in many countries of the world, but their biggest joy was sharing the love of God with others.

If there was ever a man who was a lover of souls, it was Bob Stewart. If there was ever a wife who backed her husband up in his God given call it was Ethel Stewart, a wisp of a woman with a tenacity and winsomeness that was awesome. – Brian & Dawn Hadfield

Author's note:

In the 1990's Mum shared with me several times how she felt unqualified for everything and that she had no skills at all, but that she had tried to do what she could wherever she was placed.

She loved Jesus her Savior and Lord.
She read and meditated on God's Word.
She looked after little children.
She had the gift of hospitality.
She had a generous spirit.
She was a prayer warrior.

Sometimes us four Stewart siblings have wondered where we would be and what we'd be doing today if we'd grown up in a "normal" home in the United States instead of living in three different countries.

What would it have been like to have a typical background – such as growing up in a family atmosphere? What is it like to live in the same house with parents, brothers, and sisters, or having uncles, aunts and cousins in close proximity?

In this day and age I wonder how many families do NOT have some type of dysfunctionality for we are all humans with faults and our own agendas, and all long for "normalcy, and not to be thought different."

Well MK's, otherwise known as missionary kids, are in most aspects just like any other children - needing the same love and encouragement. Their challenge comes from not knowing where they fit in society. Many have been brought up immersed in another culture - and a foreign country to boot, which they accepted as home. When it is time to return to their parent's homeland they often struggle to survive in its alien-ness.

The government of Western Australia eventually closed the aboriginal community of Cundeelee, ordered all missionaries to leave and later relocated the aborigines to Coonana. The cost ran into the millions of dollars.

Older tribal members say Coonana lacks the "soul" both of the interior and their old culture. On the other hand to them Cundeelee retains the fragrance of the good God who loves them.

Today at Cundeelee there is little evidence that any buildings ever existed. What really counts is the continuing fragrance of the Love of God that now dwells in the hearts and lives of many aborigines.

Aborigines said Bob Stewart made these tracks in 1959. photo taken in 2002

Darlene & Destiny

She was timid, shy, and poor of health,
He's given it all, and friends are her wealth.

One of the blessings of being the firstborn in our family was the close bond I had with our parents and grandparents.

I treasure memories of those times when our tiny two-bedroom home was just across the alley from Dad's parents. I excitedly watched him build a hutch so we could raise rabbits in our backyard - unaware that they would be used for food not as pets, and 'helped' Mother keep them clean. I was right there when Grandma was preserving plums and pears from our trees.

I remember dyeing eggs at Easter and wearing a new bonnet to the church that was right across the street from mother's aunt. By my seventh birthday, I would readily tell anyone who asked me that when I grew up I would be a missionary nurse in Africa. That was long before our parents had any idea of their future.

To relate the story of our parents without allowing you to see the hurdles they overcame would be to deprive you of the reality. I witnessed the responses of our parents when people around did not understand the grip of God's hand around their hearts. They were steadfast not obstinate, and obedient rather than foolhardy.

If it had been only their own idea, I am sure our parents would have turned back at the Canadian border just days into their Abraham-like journey. That was just the first of many occasions when to turn around and go home would have been a much easier option.

In Canada, Mother rubbed charcoal around our eyes before we went out to play in the snowdrifts to prevent snow-blindness. I learned Dad's weekly spelling list with him. I was fascinated watching our parents poring over the prophecies of Daniel to make accurate charts of historical events. During winter, Dad put large stones in our oven to heat ready to warm our beds at night.

Bible memorization was a key component of the curriculum at Prairie Grade School. Anyone who learned 600 verses from the Bible in one year could go to Gull Lake Bible Camp free. The year I qualified, I fell down into our root cellar spraining both ankles less than a week before camp began. Oh yes, I went – and that week I made a public commitment to serve the Lord.

I can still see Dad leading our family devotions. First, he would read the selection in Daily Light. Then we might be expected to complete a verse by memory or to suggest how we thought the selection related to us as a family.

If one of us was brave enough to ask whether a current problem meant that we were going to leave and go back to America, Dad's unwavering response was, "Any man having put his hand to the plough and looking back is not fit for the kingdom of God."

It was more than a verse he read in the Bible - it was his statement of purpose. Dad spoke those words repeatedly - at the table - to our mother as they prayed together before going to sleep - to congregations of people on both sides of the Pacific Ocean - when instructing new believers and when challenging disheartened ministers or missionaries.

Whatever the current problem, our parents prayed about it together. Often Mother would have just read a verse that was on the very topic of their concern.

Their confidence in God did not waver. If we needed rain, or money, or an operation for mother, or favor with government officials, or solution to a building problem, or wisdom to settle a dispute, or jobs for aborigines, anything at all – Dad knew that God would provide what he required.

Dad was not out to make a name for himself. He had no hidden agenda. In going to Canada to attend Bible School, it was neither to take his wife from her family, nor to upset either set of his children's grandparents. Alienation of family members was the last thing he expected. Naively he thought everyone would understand and would rejoice with him. But when they didn't, he sought comfort by reading his Bible and praying for strength to go on.

Some people stood aside to watch before passing judgment. Others shook their heads in disbelief, horror and yes, fear and made every effort to dissuade them. While others fell to their knees in prayer, put their hands in their pockets and helped in a variety of practical ways.

A patchwork quilt bearing the surnames of church members lay on our parents' bed for many years. It was a daily reminder of a dedicated group that was praying and more than one spot is tear-stained.

As time drew near for our parents to begin a second 'tour of duty', the same group arranged a Tupperware party without telling Mother their intention to send her back with all the dust-proof storage containers she could use. The items so surprisingly paid for that day by those women remained in Mother's kitchens for more than twenty-five years.

I have lasting memories of hearing our parents praying for each of us by name night after night. They were concerned about my health and my lack of friends. Knowing I anticipated becoming a missionary made them pray about where would be the best place for the necessary training.

Our parents did not discuss adult or mission matters with us. However many a night I overheard their earnest prayers. Mother's voice was soft but Dad had to speak loudly because of her deafness.

What kept them at Cundeelee were words. Jesus' words, "Other sheep I have which are not of this fold, them also I must bring and there shall be one fold and one shepherd." Then the words of men and women of like mind who followed their Savior in his search for those he referred to as 'lost sheep' provided inspiration and encouragement time and again. Hudson Taylor, Amy Carmichael, L E Maxwell, A W Tozer, F B Meyer, Charles Finney - their messages and testimonies were invaluable.

For the aborigines who were born nearby, Cundeelee was home with its familiar places, trees, and trails. It was a hallowed place full of treasured memories.

For aborigines arriving from other districts it became a place of learning to cope with transition. They faced complex issues they had never had to consider. It was a place of unexpected changes and loss of much that was familiar.

Native welfare officers saw only an isolated outpost manned by idealistic young whites who thought they could make a difference for Australia's indigenous people. Generally considered sub-human, aborigines were restricted in where they could live, provided with a minimum of water and food, and reluctantly granted access to medical care. It was just enough to keep them from media attention.

For the God-sent ones, Cundeelee became a melting pot of concerned young people. Dedicated and determined they had responded from different churches and different nations to the plight of Australia's original inhabitants. They worked together despite their differences with a sense of God's call on their lives.

Some were single; a few were couples with young children. They had left good jobs, caring families, supportive church groups to come and share the love of God with a people group whom had not heard of His love. However, here they found themselves living in sub-standard accommodation, far from medical care, without adequate or safe water, unable to get cool in summer or warm in winter. In addition to that, they were despised by government officers, feared by aboriginals, and forgotten by friends.

Mail meant contact with distant loved ones. We would wait up long past normal bedtime to see if there were any overseas letters. It took such a long time to get an answer even when the recipient wrote a reply and posted it the same day. Maintaining family awareness was not easy. Dad found it too emotional and readily delegated to Mother the responsibility of writing to family members and praying friends.

Missionaries needed to dig for water, to build houses from corrugated iron or stone, to drive and maintain old vehicles, to teach women how to recognize when their baby was dehydrated.

We could do nothing about the fact that this was an 'us and them' situation. The white missionaries lived in non-mobile structures scattered around the top of a low hill with a personal tank of water each. Aborigines lived in the shelter of a few tree branches over which a blanket or tarpaulin was thrown, which they moved every 10-14 days.

Each of our homes had a separate tiny building that we had to carefully search for red-backed spiders, centipedes and snakes before sitting on the seat over a deep hole. The aborigines had designated areas outside of their campsite that everyone used, digging a personal hole and covering it each time. When the elders determined that the firewood and sanitation situations demanded it, or when someone died, everyone would move – perhaps by 200 yards, perhaps by two miles.

Missionary mothers did what mothers everywhere did. They prepared meals; washed, hung, mended, and ironed clothes; scrubbed cement floors; attended to the physical, educational, and spiritual needs of their children; encouraged their husband, and assisted in whatever else they might find to do. Sunday school teaching to children of all ages became a challenge as well as a thrill.

When we first arrived at Cundeelee, I was eleven and wanted to help doing something, anything. All the water for the aborigines was in a 1,000-gallon water tank in the center of the mission compound. It had no tap, so each morning all the women would come with their one to two quart billycans. When everyone arrived and packed the cans side by side, Dad would bring a long black hose and start the water flowing from the tank. Then I filled each container.

The process took about an hour, depending on how many cans there were. When each woman's cans were full, she would position a coil of cloth on her head and hoist the largest one up to it. Then she would pick up her child and secure him to her back in a cloth before bending to lift a billycan in each hand. I occasionally overfilled someone's can as I watched in fascination, but a quick cry would bring me back to the task in hand.

Insects seemed to love me and created repeated traumas for my parents. First, it was something in my ear. Someone was sure that a few drops of warm olive oil would float the insect out. Sure enough, a tiny spider was glad to escape into my hair.

Not long after that, while still living in the Quonset house with dirt floor, I woke up one night with a stinging pain below my shoulder. I sat up screaming in pain and fear. Something had bitten me. Was I going to die? Dad and Mother came running.

To treat me they had to know what had bitten me. They woke Marilyn who shared my bed, and slowly searched our bedding. Finally, as they flipped the mattress, they saw a shadow. Too little to be a snake, not a spider or a scorpion, they were almost certain I would not die. A paste of bicarbonate of soda gradually relieved the pain. But I was reluctant to return to bed, even after they'd located and killed the seven inch long centipede.

Swallowing a fly while you are talking is not pleasant either, although it does make for quite a lot of laughter for those watching, especially if you swallow it!

I was ironing one night when I had a strange sense that something was in the room that should not be there. I stood very still while searching the room. Suddenly I saw a very large dark object on the mirror - a huntsman spider as big as my open hand. Mother, reluctant to leave her task in another room, calmly suggested that I step on it. That was not an option! Without taking my eyes from the monster lest it disappear, I sidled to the cupboard for the 3-lb powdered milk tin we had emptied earlier.

Carefully and quickly, I placed the can against the mirror over the spider. Holding the can with one hand and the mirror with the other, and ready to jump if I fumbled it, I moved to the table. Now it is one thing to catch a spider, and something else to dispose of it. Should I let it go outside - and run the risk of finding it later in my bed? Not likely!

An appropriate amount of methylated spirits did the trick while I made sure it did not have a companion lurking anywhere. We measured it in the morning - 5 1/2 inches.

I spent almost ten years at Cundeelee, first as the adolescent daughter of this special couple and then as one of their colleagues. As such I've watched and listened as Christian men and women learned to cry out to God knowing that He was the only one who could provide meaningful answers to their pain and questions.

Each of us knew God had assigned us to that place for that time. We were confident He would give us the strength, wisdom, and grace necessary so we could fulfill His purpose in that appointment. Success, excitement, or thrills were not our experiences. When our Commander reassigned us, most of us still had questions.

I was invited to Cundeelee in 1963 to assist Mother in caring for the six littlies. The mission board approved my application and I arrived there in August. A week later, I was dumbfounded to have Dad notify me that the nurse was leaving in 48 hours and that I would now be responsible to fill her role and to care for eight pre-teen aboriginal girls.

I protested to my father and I protested to God that I had not trained as a nurse. I did not understand enough Wangkai to hear or to speak with my aboriginal family. I had not had time to be able to identify them. I was unfamiliar with the medicines. However, neither of them seemed to be listening to me. I had no time to sit and feel sorry for myself. I went to the nurse and found out all I could while she and her husband packed.

To say that the next three years were challenging would be a serious understatement. God sometimes calls us to a task that is so much beyond us that we have to rely on Him in previously undreamed-of ways.

How thankful I am that God did not abandon me to work things out for myself. He assured me of His presence. Then He opened my heart and my ears to these precious people. Repeatedly when I did not know what to do and could not get in touch with a doctor, I would sense God's nudge – and, it worked!

I also gained incredible support from the Royal Flying Doctor that provides a service to remote inland areas of Australia that is second to none. Everyone appreciates the pilots and doctors, who take time from their own private practices to meet distant emergencies.

I was wondering if I would ever be relieved of my duties when God sprang a surprise on me. His plan for my life was about to come to a 90deg turn. Three years previously, He had whispered to Bob Kingi, a native of New Zealand, a secret that would affect both of our lives.

But that is another story. It is enough to say that all of us had to get ready for the changes that would follow my 'Yes' to the itinerant evangelist's proposal.

Dad and Mother were never ones to stand in the way of God's purposes in a person's life. Nowhere was that shown better than in their support of our marriage that would take me away from Cundeelee. The oneness of heart shared there we maintained over the years, in spite of the distances that would once again separate us.

* * *

Bob and Darlene moved to New Zealand in 1971 and have been blessed with four children and a granddaughter.

One son passed away in 1983 and her husband joined him in heaven in 1992.
God continues to surprise Darlene with unexpected tasks that require His enabling. At the request of her church leaders, she was ordained as a minister and spent the last five years pastoring a small church.
Darlene enjoys sharing the practicalities of living one's faith with women's groups.

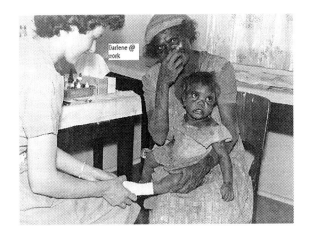

Bob & Ethel Stewart

Stephen, Marilyn, Dale, Darlene

Dale & Duty

**Some yarns I'll share – no worries, just a few –
Memories of old, yet they seem ever new.**

Every kid needs something to lay claim to. For some it was all the marbles, for others athletic supremacy. Most of my playmates excelled at tracking or hunting, and a few tended to be great dreamers. I guess you could say I fit into most categories a little, but in the last one, I excelled.

Memories for me are mostly like that of a cloud floating overhead. One minute I am watching it float along, the next it dulls the sunny day, then in another minute or so it moves on and becomes another thing stored in my memory of past history. There were the rockholes, snakes, lizards, and spiders, the temperamental old army generator and at night, cats screeching as they slid down the corrugated rooftops.

I remember things like splitting railroad sleepers (ties), playing cricket, and spinning on our discarded camel cartwheel (merry-go-round), as well as the Saturday hunting hike. There was the day that a snoozing big red kangaroo was startled awake and leaping up "flew" right over the head of Don Sinclair. Memories of being careful when we explored as some of the areas that seemed so intriguing were forbidden territory to women and children as well as uninitiated boys.

Early on, we had school by correspondence and School of the Air via our short-wave radio 9EK. Our Quonset hut home had no electricity so we often did our lessons in almost unbearable heat or chilled to the bone. Teachers never seemed to stay too long, and at one stage we even traveled 26 miles (one way) to attend school at Zanthus.

I will never forget those camp feeds, or the Sunday all-in-one-meal in huge cauldrons over an open fire and the resulting scorched taste if Dad preached too long.

In memory, I watch a storm build and recall standing outside with Dad watching lightning strike an old tree 4 or 5 miles away. Then hearing him tiredly sigh and say we best fill the barrels with water, gather all the shovels, and burlap sacks for tomorrow early we will be out fighting that fire.

A vivid and painful memory is of our leaving the outback in 1956 - of promising to return, only to learn in 1957 that I would be left behind in a completely different foreign country.

I was an insecure 16-year-old boy in a strange land with nothing familiar to cling to. The nights were the worst for the inner turmoil boiled over from my thoughts into my dreams and I wondered if I would ever find another place in which my soul would quiet and feel at home.

I knew nothing of work permits, passports, visas, draft boards, mandatory military service or a zillion other things that were common knowledge to my peers. I only knew of heartbreak, loneliness, missing family members, of nowhere I could call home or of anything or person I could grasp onto for security. I had no one to talk to and my thoughts and feelings were pulsating with adventure, insecurity, fears of all kinds, girls, and of course cars!

My father had taught me the importance of honoring my word and the value or binding agreement it held. I was stunned to learn through sad experience, that just because a businessman claimed to be a Christian it didn't always mean he could be trusted to be a man of his word.

Joining the service was a turning point in my life. The reasons I had for joining up seemed good at the time, and would prove to open an entirely new world of opportunities to me. I learned discipline, experienced many hardships, and also began to build self esteem and skills. Once while on maneuvers, I remembered an event from my childhood and was able to re-enact it with delightful results.

I was a great dreamer who needed a quiet secure place of my own. My space or time capsule became "the tree".

Before Dad picked the building site for our home I had selected this particular tree as my very own. It was a most unusual tree for it was very large. At some point in time the core of it had rotted, ants had taken over and proceeded to fill the cavity with clay. Over the years, the clay had hardened until it was now as hard as cement.

The task I set for myself was to evict the tenants (ants) and remove their fortress, which measured about three feet wide by five feet high - without the benefit of metal tools. Neither Mum nor Dad was willing to let me borrow any implements when I would not tell them what I needed them for – it was my secret. Actually, it was a secret I shared with my friend Peter Jamieson, a bush boy I was supposed to be helping to learn English. There were several reasons that our project took a year to complete and one factor was the effort I/we put in to keep it a secret.

Before we began our venture Peter and I were virtual out-casts, but every time we tried to slip away unnoticed just like magic there would be someone tracking us. We would detour here and there, for what seemed like hours then blot out our tracks and like a pair of ghosts slip away.

In later years I found out - they were simply trying to find out to what lengths we would go to during our escape and evasion, to keep them from our secret place. Even worse was the news that my partner with his limited vocabulary in English and mine in Wangkai did not understand that it was a secret and so had, unwittingly, sold me out.

Our hollowed out tree was a masterpiece of excavation and eviction, and provided many hours of solitude. We could sit high above the ground hidden by the leafy camouflage, with quick access to the escape chute into the interior of the tree trunk if escape became necessary. During the times I sat, or sometimes studied, I would dream of days yet to come when I might be the one that through vigilance might save my small world.

Many years later, on countless military guard posts, those memories helped pass the hours. On those cold lonely nights, there were times I would have given anything to have been back within the comfort and security of that tree's protection.

Interestingly enough, while on military exercises during a pouring rainstorm, another soldier and I discovered an old stump. It was seven or eight feet tall, five feet across, with a completely rotten core. Within a short period of time we had removed the rotten material, buried it under the natural surrounding cover, and camouflaged the top. We were concealed so well that when our Lieutenant came searching for us we were able to sneak up behind him. Later we showed him this great hiding place, which afforded us a terrific field for observation and fire. As well as that, we were the only two soldiers to have a dry place to rest during the times we were not on lookout.

One of the best memories I have from my return visit in '92 was the discovery that my childhood escape place is alive and well, and just as I remember it.

* * *

Abundance - it is more than just a word!

Sundays were always combination days, the combination being no work, or play. So for kids it meant, church, then soup or stew from huge cauldrons cooked over a fire, and depending on the long windedness of the preacher, usually dad, it was either ok, or burnt on the bottom. Funny thing about burned food – even though it only burned the bottom of the pot the whole pot of food was affected.

One Sunday we had decided to fix food at home since mum was sick. On this day, since Darlene was off at school, dad took over the cooking. A week previously when dad had met the tea & sugar (supply) train he had seen and purchased something he was sure mum would like – some of the new "self-rising" flour. That day seemed like the perfect day to try it out.

What we were having besides potatoes and gravy I cannot recall, nor in the scope of ensuing events does it amount to much. What I do recall is that the gravy began to grow, and the more he stirred the more it expanded. Soon dad asked for another pan, then another, and it seemed as if the miracle of the five loaves and two fishes was about to happen all over again, except there was no multitude to feed, just kids laughing at the plight of our dad, the COOK.

The lesson here escaped me for many years until I was teaching a class and that incident came to mind when trying to explain about the abundance of God's great love and mercy. All analogies break down as this one does in that eventually the gravy had overflowed the final pan, whereas God's abundant love and mercy toward us sinners is endless.

* * *

Dale is married, has a grown daughter, and lives with his wife in the Pacific Northwest.

Dale's Tree

Poem & Present

Years have past; still we struggle, in learning how to cope
With white culture, English, and even using soap.
Instead of using hair, we see a strong thick rope,
And a truck that moves faster, than we can even lope.
In winter we now have a warm blanket for a coat;
Hard to keep our ancient culture, still, we find a little hope.

A few are being noticed, Aborigines with a "name" –
An Artist; Musicians, and a Runner gaining fame.
Artifacts that sell, and dot paintings are the game –
But underneath all this, nothing changes, all the same.
Diabetes now runs rampant, we are halt, and we are lame –
Human nature and agendas seem impossible to tame.

2004 hope dims, as it is still them, and us;
We live on the fringes of towns, in the dust.
Companies eye and mine our lands with lust;
All we're asking for is what is fair, and just
We have served, labored, tracked, and still lack your trust;
To heal our land, listen to our voice, is simply a must.

Marilyn Stewart

Marilyn & Musing

**I hope you've enjoyed these stories with me –
To grow in faith - obedience is key.**

From my point of view, the past is the past and if I choose to dwell too long there I lose the present NOW and all of my future NOWS lying ahead.

As the Spinifex aborigines taught me many years ago – neither the past nor the future feed me today.

Today is the day to feed me for the future, whether it is literal food for my physical body, a change in my attitude for the well being of the inner me, or in learning something new in order to improve my mind.

I never dreamt of writing a book – let alone two!

I am not a confident writer. I struggle with grammar, run-on sentences and apostrophes in the wrong places. Writing for me is a four-letter word – WORK.

Right now, I am writing – yes, with old-fashioned tools – a pencil and paper. Later I will use the computer and spell check.

This past year I decided to join a writers group. After the first meeting, I was invited to bring some of my books (*Child of the Outback*) to sell at our next meeting.

I have never been so intimidated in my life as when I knew that writers would be reading my book - not even being on live TV! Most of them had published hundreds of articles and a few – books.

At the second meeting, I sold a few and then lived in fear of attending the next meeting. I knew my skin was not thick enough for too many pithy comments, but I wanted to learn to write better. As I left the car headed for class, I grabbed a few more books - just in case no one had read it and someone else wanted a copy. Before rounding the corner I wiped my sweating hands on my slacks, took a deep breath, made sure my smile was in place before stepping in the door.

The person in charge greeted me with the words – "Just one thing wrong with your book! There is nowhere in it that states what else you've written." I blinked and wanted to howl with laughter, but calmly replied, "I've never written anything else." It was now their turn to look at me blankly.

You see all the writing has been a God driven thing and I am as surprised as anyone that He chose and gifted me to do it. Maybe the following poem will explain my feelings.

My life had hurts – not all bliss,
Many times I'd reflected on things I'd missed.
The Lord said, "Marilyn, what is in your fist?
Opening it slightly I saw my "wants" list.

He said, "Write, and on negatives don't dwell,
I thought - this is not something I desire to tell.
But, I wrote my book, and no publisher would sell,
I wanted to cheer, to jump up and yell.

Then – "Print on Demand will publish your book."
Our bank account, Lord – would you just take a look!
We scraped up the cash, pinching each penny it took,
He'd given me the background, the bait, now the hook.

You want me to do what, Lord? I cried!
Talk to people, and swallow my pride?
I'll sell my book, but from an audience hide,
Then I saw His hands, stretching out and open wide.

From living as a barefoot outback child to talking to hundreds of people - it has been an amazing journey. I figured I had written my one book and was never going to have to struggle with sentence structure again. Yippee!

And then came along another assignment – another compulsion to get these stories told. Time and again I would lay the pages out and say, "Okay Lord, this is your doing! I am totally out of my depth. I am discouraged for the task is too large for me. I cannot seem to get an ending for this chapter, for this book," and on and on I would go!

Ah, the Lord was so good to me!

In case you missed them during your reading – here are some of the outstanding things that took place during the writing of this book.

In February, my brother Stephen related something that had happened just that week, which perfectly finished the chapter I was working on titled Footprints & Fragrance.

In March, my sister Darlene sent me a letter written by our father in 1967 that was not only the perfect ending to a talk I was giving in April, but also for this book.

In May, my brother Dale sent me a photo of the first written (printed) words in the Wangkai language. I needed it.

In June, Roger Green sent me the letter regarding the first inland trip. (I had laid that chapter out and prayed over it numerous times, as it just was not quite right.) The very week that I decided, it was time to knuckle down and seriously tear it apart – I received the information I needed. It has been an amazing thing to watch His hand at work.

In July, Brian Hadfield e-mailed me, about words [vocabulary section] and my tjamu, Willy. It was exactly what I needed - it also forced me to completely rewrite the chapter I had half written and named Coolgobin & Carlene.

During the night hours came not only the title - Wonders & Words, but also how to fit it all together.

While writing this book there have been three major times that I have thought, "This is too hard. I want to quit. Let my sister who writes better than I do write it."

And each time for a few days I did quit - until I had a change of attitude. I started to change my focus by saying, "Amaze/Astonish me today, Father - may you be glorified." Then each day I watch for His hand at work.

A sentence came together.

He gave me a faithful prayer partner.

An encouraging e-mail from someone I'd never met.

A creative writing teacher said, "You have a real gift." (I still laugh in amusement/shock at that one!)
An unexpected card came in the mail.
Three people offered help in editing it!
The topping on the cake so to say came when Darlene was able to come for a month in Nov. and helped with the final editing – lots of dashes are gone as are run on sentences. She had some added insights we were able to incorporate into some stories.

When placed with the creator, of the sea and the land,
A little boy's lunch more than grew – it did expand.
To each of us here he asks – what is in your hand?
Yielding what we hold, can release His larger plan.

Marilyn Stewart

If you would like to read about my life's journey in detail, from barefoot and hunting for my food to snow and culture shock, you can go to www.buybooksontheweb.com and preview/order *Child of the Outback.*

2002

Stephen & Society

**Given the name, Nyndi at a young age was I,
Still live in the outback under the bright blue sky.**

My earliest memories are of playing in the aboriginal camp with my mates - Robbie, Lindsay, Lesley, Peter, Norman, Arnold, and Cyril. I will always appreciate Mr. & Mrs. Peddler, surrogate missionary parents, for their generosity towards me. The Franks and McCarthy families were especially important and hold key places in my heart.

Aboriginal women offered to care for me during school hours along with their own little children. Mother gratefully accepted. When they took a nap, I took a nap. When they had lunch so did I – whatever it might be: roasted lizard, damper with jam, or witchetty grubs and always, billy tea. It was in camp that I spoke my first word: Nyndi – meaning to know or understand. I'm told that on the spot the elders excitedly designated this word to me as a fitting Wangkai name.

When the women were not looking after me, Dad took me with him in the truck. Sometimes we would go to Zanthus and meet the Tea-and-Sugar train. We would wait for hours for it to arrive and I'd be rewarded by being allowed to make my own purchase of a Violet Crumble Bar. When I was a little older Don, Colin, Johnny, and Ralph would take me with them to collect sandalwood or firewood.

I remember Mum sitting with a group of women as they crocheted hats and Dad leaving to go bush, returning with more strangers – and sporting a beard. Most of all I remember being surrounded by aboriginal people – always.

I used to use the word "sacrifice" when referring to the hardships and disappointments experienced by our family. But, when I think of the sacrifice that God made to deal with the conflict between good and evil, and put our experiences into this perspective, I come to the conclusion that I don't know what sacrifice means.

Many who read books about the lives of other people wonder if it was worth it all. It depends on what you are looking for. In affluent societies, money is their basis. Success is measured by how much money one has to use or to invest and how quickly one can get more.

But what determines the worth of a people group to whom money or any concept of purchase is completely foreign? Is it the monetary value they are able to return to the dominant culture? Is it how they hold their own culture together? Is it whether they can manage to let go of their own traditions and learn to compromise? I believe it is the intrinsic worth of each diverse group irrespective of the monetary value of their possessions.

The federal government funds most indigenous communities in Australia these days. This came as a result of a new conscience toward its collective responsibility for attitudes that resulted in the displacement of an ancient culture. However, in funding these communities, the government makes no commitment to their long-term support. Part of the reason for this is that they do not recognize the existence of the system of laws and responsibilities that are still being practiced by traditional aboriginal groups.

These codes of practice have been in place for as long as this ethnic group has existed, and they cannot be changed arbitrarily without seriously affecting their entire culture. Even an outside group appointed by a federal government body would have to engage in serious and genuine consultation with all people that are governed by those laws before initiating wholesale changes.

A judge recently told me that the aboriginal culture was an inferior one and that they really have no option but to give in to our laws and system.

Having spent most of my life among these people, I am of a different opinion. Their system of laws and responsibilities, as rudimentary as it may seem to the casual observer, is nonetheless a functioning government.

Yet Aboriginal people are very much under white Australian laws, paying taxes to both the federal and state governments. They are not exempt. Neither, is their right to occupy their own land, guaranteed to them, because the government, having the final say, - regards it as crown land.

So much is said about our relatives of different color and culture that I balk at writing anything at all. My struggle is that unless I can get you to understand something of their point of view, this will not benefit them at all. I feel obligated to do this because people usually interpret the actions that are presented in print, movies, and human observation in a stereotyped way.

My contribution to this book is to try to show that this primitive people have a living breathing culture that is being attacked from every side and needs to be protected.

In the last fifty years, I have witnessed much loss with the passage of traditional customs and the resulting changes within this culture. The influence of western culturalization has left in its wake a people that are powerless to deal with the law and order issues that now face their communities.

Gradually agencies have taught this isolated group that they must show their worth if they are to be funded. They must show off their uniqueness by encouraging tourism and producing artifacts and paintings to sell. Younger members must leave their community and find meaningful employment in town or city. If the maintenance of one's culture is not a fulltime meaningful occupation, what is?

Government bodies have taken the position that tourism of necessity includes guiding strangers into their homeland and revealing sacred locations to them. This is seen to be an acceptable means of acquiring an income.

However, indigenous peoples of the world have westerners worked out, and those living in isolated desert communities are no different. This cultural group is an open society. They see right through insincerity and hidden agendas. [*Until recently, they did not even hide behind clothes. Even today in a fight all clothes are removed - not only to stop from being hampered by loose garments, but also as a statement of integrity: "This is me you can all see my whole body naked before you. As sure as I am standing here like this and you can see me, I assure you that I am not covering up anything. Now this is the statement I make."]*

They watch the visitors who arrive uninvited and unannounced - like a bowling ball in the midst of whatever is in progress - without regard for good manners or local protocol. Should there be a card game in progress, where money is being wagered, the visitors often censure the players. If the locals were less polite they would point out a few home truths to their judges.

While they may be losing a few dollars to one another, what about westerners' socially acceptable ways of losing lots of money? Government schemes obliging involvement with the stock market, banks that have peoples' money tied up in investments that lately have lost money. They are aware of gambling in the form of Lotto, in casinos, and now the hidden form – on the internet.

This ancient tradition allows people to see everything so they do not consider themselves to be above others. They see each shortcoming and everyone talks about it. True, it doesn't make it right, but my point is that those who secretly indulge ought not to despise those who openly indulge.

Let's talk about their code of practice. Although there is not a king/queen hierarchy, there are rules of acceptable behavior. According to traditional cultural procedures, misdeeds are punished in a way that fits the crime.

Decisions are made at meetings where Elders thrash out and determine the correct position to take on a matter. No one person makes any decision – it is the collective responsibility. The Elders dictate who is allowed to go and where and when. Whether or not one thinks it's a fair system, is not the point. The Elders have spoken.

Sadly, the indigenous people of this area have lost all the Elders that came in from the bush and will soon have lost the Elders that were young men or boys at that time. It is a sad fact that the current Elders do not hold firmly to the protocols of their immediate predecessors. Even now the whims of the younger generation (30-50 year olds) are beginning to dictate what amount of involvement they will have, and when, and for how long.

Future Elders will be Elders only in age not in the true sense of the traditional word understood by the tribal men of the Spinifex era. If the younger men who are now responsible for the sacred traditions of the past do not have a radical mind shift, the significance of this culture will, in future, only be read about in schoolbooks.

To me the modern shift is a sign that little regard is held for the uniqueness of the core of the culture. As recently as 20-25 years ago, there was no option. Men took part in the traditional activities or they left, joined themselves to a different culture, and did not return. That was the way it was.

Some young aborigines are glad that it is being eroded. They are aware that under their ancient laws they would not be able to talk about anything regarding tradition until they earned the right to do so. Very few aboriginal town dwellers or tourist operators are strong lawmen. They are considered to be children in the eyes of their own tradition and have not been entrusted with the secrets reserved for fully initiated men. Their own tradition strictly forbids them to discuss any issue regarding their laws and observances.

It stands to reason that one cannot be a custodian of any sacred or significant land if he is forbidden from knowing exactly where it is and what was done there. He would not be authorized by the tribal elders to care for it. If he were caught in that restricted area, he and/or his parents would certainly suffer because of his flagrant disregard for the laws of their society.

The older women too have Laws they are responsible to safeguard. Areas designated of special significance to women are out of bounds to male persons. They may not go anywhere near those locations. The fact that it was his mother's country does not give a man the right to visit it – much less take anyone else to it.

If this culture is to survive and thrive these observances must be protected by traditional Lawmen and women. What is the message for the group of people that make up the culture of which we are so much a part? How can we best encourage people of every cultural background?

Some of you are wondering about Christian perspectives and how the message of the Bible applies to this culture. I believe that each individual is responsible for his own relationship with the Giver of life.

The message to this and any culture is that Almighty God is both gracious and just. While He loves us, God is bound by His own judicial system. If we sin, and it is a certainty we will, according to His Word God is faithful and just to forgive our sins every time we repent. He allows us the opportunity of a "do over" a new start.

No matter what society you belong to there are attitudes and lifestyles that are tolerated - whether it is pride or affluence, jealousy or greed - whatever sets you up as being better than your fellow man.

In relation to the gospel, all men are created equal. No one is less or more deserving of God's free gift of salvation than anyone else. All mankind has sinned and requires redemption through Jesus Christ. Once we have accepted this relationship with God, then our response is to ensure that others are given the opportunity to understand God's provision of forgiveness and union with the Creator.

So do I consider what my parents regarded as profoundly important as having achieved good outcomes? This I know: my parents were faithful in sharing the Good News of the Gospel to a race of people that they were convinced needed to hear this most important message. In a sense my parents' destiny was and is wrapped up in the personal relationship they each have with the provider of this act of Grace for all mankind.

Was it worth all the pain and separation from family? Absolutely! Their personal love for God the Father was their motivation. I know this because I, more than most, witnessed their wholehearted dedication. Do I resent this preoccupation as having robbed me of family time together? No. I have seen families that are together where there is as much heartache as there is with those that have not had the opportunity of closeness.

In conclusion, I am not to know what your relationship is with Jesus, let alone your family. But, please do not hold God responsible for anything that was done to you or was not done for you - even if that person was a Christian. God is the ultimate judge – leave them to Him.

Now it is between you and God. God holds each of us individually accountable for our time spent here on earth. Deal with it! Then LIVE!

What prevents us from accepting this most wonderful gift? It is our will. We choose to act in certain ways whether it is mental attitudes or other sins. Perhaps this is the time to seriously consider your position before Jesus Christ. Have you accepted this free gift that we refer to?

God's invitation is to you as an individual. In the solitude of your thoughts, you can respond to the offer that He has made. No fuss, no fanfare - just respond to the call of the Holy Spirit as He awakens your soul to this message of forgiveness and hope.

Stephen is in the left corner with Spotty.

Stephen has recently remarried, still lives in Australia, has three children and three grandchildren.

1959 - 1st time for billy tea and damper

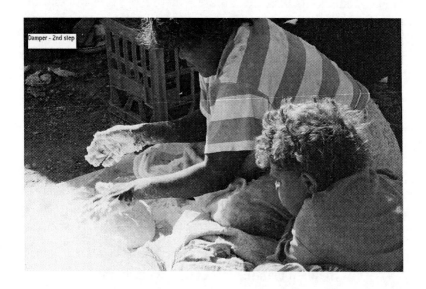

Damper - 2nd step

Recipes

Billy Tea

Fire
Billy (a can - with a handle is preferred)
Water
¼ cup of tea leaves (a handful – more or less)

Bring the water in the billy to a rolling boil, remove the billy (can) from the fire, toss in the tea leaves and wait for it to brew. (Do not like the smoky taste? Find a tin with a lid and boil the water with the lid on.)
Pour into mugs and add sugar and milk to taste.

* * *

Whenever we had a school teacher we had a morning "tea" break, and the kids would get a drink of milk/Milo mixture. I remember helping to prepare it – after an adult had punched the holes in the cans.

1 large metal bucket
2 cans of canned milk – opened and poured into bucket
Add several scoops of Milo - mix very well!
One person stirred while the other added water until the bucket was full
(If the water had just finished boiling for the required twenty minutes then you had a hot or warm drink – otherwise it was a warm drink in summer and cold in winter.)

Damper

1 cup of Self-Rising flour
A generous pinch of Salt
¼ cup (or a little less) of water
(too much makes it tough)
Lots of hot coals and warm ashes

Mix flour, salt and water (on a floured gunnysack)
Place and gently flatten out mixture in bottom of camp oven or on a lightly greased foil sheet (in place of an oven) – loosely pull up edges to completely cover the damper.

Make a depression in the hot coals and place oven or foil right on top of them. Pull the hot coals over the tin foil or place them on the lid of the camp oven.

Coals too hot – outside burnt inside raw
Not cooked long enough - rubbery
Will almost double in size
Cooking time about 45 minutes

- If you are very well off you can add an egg
- No oven or foil? No worries! Just flour the dough a little extra before placing in the coals and cook, but dust off the ashes before consuming.

Vocabulary

Billycan	a can used to carry water & brew tea
Damper	campers' bread – without yeast
Dogger	a hunter of dingoes
Karlkurla	wild pear (or bush bananas)
Kulila	listen or pay attention
Kunmanu	no name
Kurta	brother
Ngayulu	in reference to me, but means "I"
Mamakuurti	the good Father Spirit (God)
Marlu	red kangaroo
Milo	a drink similar to Ovaltine
Mulga	a tree with very hard wood
Ngaru	sorry
Pina Lyunku	ear that is blocked deaf or cannot hear
Spinifex	clumps of sharp grass like cactus needles
Tea & Sugar	slow train carried – food, water, & passengers
Tilly	a lantern - usually having a mantle rather than a wick
Tucker	food
Wardi	a stout stick 1 ½" – 2" thick and 2' – 3' long
Woomera	catapult used in throwing a spear

* * *

Brian Hadfield shared the following with me.

The comments below are made with sympathy concerning the confusion met by those who come into contact with various expressions of the written form of Aboriginal languages. It is a bit like the old British Railroad system where every company had its own track gauge.

While in England in 2000, we had the joy seeing phields (fields) phull (full) of pheasants, as we drove along. Then behold we saw pheasents phlying phrom phenses. Earlier I asked a man where the town of "Brough" [Bro] as in dough was. He looked at me strangely, and when I repeated "Bro," he snorted and said grough/ff/ly, Oh! You mean Bruff.

And so it is in a new unwritten language/dialect – it depends on the person who hears it spoken, and then when there are many dialects with similar sounds the writing of it becomes the individual's choice.

All of the following spellings are the same word: Wongi - Wangi -Wangai - Wanggai - Wangkai - Wangkayi - Wongkai – as well as Oneguy!

It is very interesting though when it comes to writing Wangkai or any Aboriginal language we tend to move toward what we hear.

Author's notes:

Many of the aboriginal words in this book are not spelled the same as in my previous book. I now have two dictionaries and often neither agrees on how to spell the same word.

And so you the reader now have an idea of the complexities of unwritten dialects and I hope will realize that whatever spelling I use someone will disagree with it.

Puppies & Perfection

**They wouldn't walk they wouldn't crawl,
All they'd do is sit and bawl.**

December 19th - We suddenly became the guardians of not one, but two small Pomeranians the color of hoarfrost. We named these brothers Cinco (five) and Seis (six) which is the number of Poms' over the years we've welcomed into our abode to "rule" our lives.

We were about to experience, up close and personal, a valuable object lesson.

We had never had two the exact same age and in the puppy stage together. They fed of each other in being playful and disobedient. Pomeranians ruling is one thing, but not puppies! At five months of age, we all went to puppy school for eight weeks.

A new class of puppies, playing, not in line –
From Pomeranians to a Beagle, the total numbered nine.
We're here to learn not to bark, pee, or whine –
But at touch, sit, heel, and stay, we hope to soon shine!
At first it was chaos, at least most of the time –
Until we learned obedience, now on treats we do dine.
Then slowly, but surely, we began to look so fine –
Till no one could tell whose butt hit first, yours or mine.
Marilyn Stewart

There were nine puppies enrolled with our two being the smallest to a Great Pyrenees, also five months of age, which began class weighing fifty pounds. The trainer said no holding them - toughen them up and make them stay on the floor - at which they scooted under our chairs all the while crying pitifully.

When the instructions were over and it was time to proceed to walk our three and four pound fluff balls, they just sat on their fannies and shivered - refusing to walk, run or even move under their own steam. The trainer said he had witnessed this type of behavior before and advised us to drag them around behind us. He was confidently that before the end of class that day they would be walking.

During each week, we were to work with our puppies twice a day for ten minutes only, and at different locations. They were coming right along with heel and sit, stay and down, provided that is they were not in the vicinity of where class was held. It was so embarrassing that they both sat or laid down the minute they got to the door and never walked another step until they were back outside once again.

Oh my, what personal lessons they were teaching us. They would do all of their lessons perfectly, but only where and when it suited them. They were the ones in charge – but no one was enjoying the experience.

Unexpectedly, late into the third class, and after at least nine visits to the store, as if responding to an unseen motion they suddenly stood up and walked.

People passing by would stop to praise them on how well they did their tricks.

On the last day of puppy school the class voted - Seis won most improved. Cinco won the musical chairs for he would sit immediately on command. They both faultlessly obeyed each command, and wove through the staggered cones perfectly. Cinco and Seis took almost all of the prizes, and they each received a diploma.

Just as in the end, the Poms made us all look good due to their trust and obedience to our commands, so God desires us to make Him look good!

It takes Faith, Trust and Obedience to His commands.